THE HISTORY OF HARLEQUIN

MR LEWIS POLWORTH AS HARLEQUIN.

London, Pub Sep^t 14, 1844, by J.K.GREEN, 16, Park Place, East Street, Walworth.

No 4.

THE HISTORY OF
HARLEQUIN

By
CYRIL W. BEAUMONT

With a Preface by
SACHEVERELL SITWELL

A Cover Design and Decorations by
CLAUDIA GUERCIO

And Illustrations from Contemporary Sources

Benjamin Blom
New York

First Published in London 1926
by Cyril W. Beaumont
Reissued 1967 by Benjamin Blom, Inc., New York 10452
By arrangement with Cyril W. Beaumont
Library of Congress Catalog Card No. 65-27909

Printed in U.S.A. by
NOBLE OFFSET PRINTERS, INC.
NEW YORK 3, N. Y.

HARLEQUIN is notoriously a difficult person to catch, but I think Mr. Beaumont has pinned him down and elicited what few facts are to be found about his career. The chase has been long and arduous, and any one who has pursued the quarry even a short distance through theatrical history disbelieves the silly theory that any of the Masks of the Italian Comedy have descent from the buffoons of the Roman stage. The region of true comedy can be perfected, but not much enlarged ; and so, given like conditions, the same types are bound to appear time after time.

Where, as I say, all the facts about Harlequin are set down, and in addition his *rôle* has been analysed and examples given of his action, I must content myself with watching his effect upon the audience, and I need not say that I choose those members of the audience that can express themselves, for a book of history has no use for mute memories. What I want to examine here, in fact, is Harlequin's effect upon artists.

There have been, of course, innumerable kinds of Harlequins ; but, as a whole, we may think of him in terms of an historical figure not inferior in importance to the Emperor Nero, or Archbishop Laud. His portrait has certainly been painted far more often than those of the entire Stuart family, and the imagination is happier in his company than in that of the Twelve Cæsars in marble and porphyry.

We can form a dim idea, perhaps, from the presence among us

of a company of dancers who have lasted for twenty years under the rule of their great impresario, of what perfections must have been reached in companies like the *Gelosi*, who existed for a couple of generations. No wonder that their arrival in France or Germany set every sensitive heart beating, and that the old became young again for an hour in the false and uncertain candlelight!

The seventeenth century was the golden age of theatrical production, as all those know who have been privileged to see *Monumenta Scenica*, the vast theatrical collection now in course of publication from Vienna. Dr. Josef Gregor, the editor of the series, places this period with the age of Pericles and the age of Shakespeare as the supreme moments in our present branch of history. Unfortunately, if we look at the works of Jacques Callot, who invented this peculiar *genre* of theatrical drawing, we find no sign of Harlequin. He came into full being a little later than Callot's day, and we must leave the Bolognese doctor, Scaramouch, Pantaloon, and the rest of them to work a little longer at their fantasies before we can find Harlequin at play among them.

This, so far at any rate as I am concerned, is sad, for I miss him not only where I have just noticed his absence, but he does not seem to have occurred much in the great age of the Machinists. There is no drawing of him in the album of *Monumenta Scenica* devoted to Burnacini, and in the heroic mazes and labyrinths of the Bibbiena family we see no sign of him.

We come upon him at last in the hands of Claude Gillot, the master of Watteau. This painter was some dozen years older than his famous pupil, and died a year later. It was from Gillot that Watteau derived his love of the stage, for during the years that he was under his influence, Gillot was a painter of scenery and decorations for the theatre, and Watteau assisted him in this work, and was by this means introduced behind the scenes. Gillot's world lay in two halves : in one he was occupied with *diableries*, scenes of satyrs and fauns, and in the other with harlequinades. Watteau, in learning from his master, neglected the former in favour of the latter, but, although he is an artist of much greater

x

stature than Gillot, the pictures of Italian comedians by Watteau
may be said to be too poetical and not enough theatrical. Watteau
takes his actors away from the theatre and places them in a park,
at the edge of a statue or fountain ; they are never painted against
their true background of canvas wall or tree. Sometimes they are
seen mingling with the guests at some great assembly in a garden,
but even here the comedians are shown sitting too much at their
ease in strange company.

Because he was painted by Watteau, Harlequin comes into the
pictures of Lancret and Pater, but his *rôle* is diminished in their
inferior hands, and we see the sentimental ghost of that rapid and
bright mask. If we want to see him in his primitive force we must
look at the illustrations to the chapter on Harlequin in P. L.
Duchartre's book on the Italian comedy.

The reign of Louis XIV., as we said some few lines back, was
the beginning of the great age of Harlequins. Biancolelli, known
as Domenico, was the first of them to reach fame ; he died in 1688
from a chill caught while dancing before the French king, and
was succeeded in his *rôle* the following year by Evaristo Gherardi.
He acted this part until 1697, and spent the next three years in
producing a collection of the pieces in which he had acted. These
may be said to be the chief authority on Harlequin, and they are
illustrated by some excellent engravings, reproduced in Duchartre's
book, showing Harlequin in his authentic world, which is very
different from that imagined for him by Watteau and the painters
of *fêtes-galantes*.

We must hold back, at this point, from being drawn into Mr.
Beaumont's province. Having made a bare mention of Gherardi,
it is difficult to refrain from continuing the succession of Harlequins
through Vicentini, known as Thomassin, Bertinazzi, called Carlin,
Sacchi, and all the rest of that daring and volatile talent. It is
painful to think of that dead world of poetry the greatness of which
we can only estimate in terms of what we have ourselves experienced. What memories are conjured up in our minds at the mere
photograph of Nellie Wallace, Little Tich, the Fratellini, or Grock ?

But Mr. Beaumont has unearthed all there is to be found, and we must content ourselves here with a collection, so to speak, of theatrical photographs.

Having returned in this manner to our portfolios, I now register one of the most sincere griefs in my recreation. Of all the painters who could ever have drawn Harlequin I would sooner see his portrait by Tiepolo than by any other hand. Yet in all the four carnival pictures by him (two of them belonged once to Princess Mathilde Bonaparte, and the other pair are still in the Papadopoli Palace in Venice) there is no sign of Harlequin. Tiepolo's favourite mask would seem to have been Pulcinella. He comes into these four pictures, was often drawn by him, and forms the actual subject of a series of etchings by his hand. Domenico Tiepolo, the son of the great artist, had the same enthusiasm. The ceiling paintings now in the Museo Correr at Venice, and which came from the Tiepolo family villa at Zianigo, on the Brenta, are the culmination in the portrayal of this particular mask, and Domenico continued this branch of his father's activity with a series of over one hundred sepia drawings of Pulcinella. Yet there are no Harlequins !

The same disappointment awaits us in the *Ridotto* pictures, those mysterious gambling scenes and conversations in the *Parlatorio* of convents, the painter of which dual subjects is unknown, though I believe critical opinion inclines to attribute them to Guardi. There are several of these pictures to be seen ; one of them belongs to Monsieur Jacques Blanche, and there are two of them in the Museo Correr and a couple in the Doria Gallery in Rome ; and in all of these among the masks in the crowd Pulcinella is to be seen, but never Harlequin. There is no Harlequin on the staircase at the Palazzo Grassi in Venice, which Pietro Longhi frescoed with a carnival scene ; and Magnasco painted a whole series of little pieces on the life of Pulcinella, which form part of the collection of Signor Italico Brass in Venice, where, once again, Harlequin does not appear. We shall see, later on, that his apparent disfavour at the hands of famous painters has been reversed in the last century.

Engravings of him by less famous artists there are in profusion. There is a series of sixteen plates and a frontispiece by G. J. Xavery, of Amsterdam, of a comedy in which Harlequin gave birth to a son, a situation that lends itself, as may be imagined, to a series of comic, if rather coarse, variations. The Dutch polders and the red-brick houses of Holland seem an unlikely background for our hero, yet we find many more instances of his career on this alien soil, a very fine, unsigned engraving of Niccolo Caccatrippa, and a pastel by Cornelius van Troost of a barber-Harlequin, which is the best work of this little-known master in the room devoted to his works at the Mauritshuis.[1] I have no access to the engravings of an earlier artist, De Geijn, but it is probable that there are Harlequins among his comedians.

Before we leave these older scenes I must mention the two things that are, in my opinion, the greatest works of art to do with the Italian theatre. First is that astounding book known, I think, to but a few theatrical students. It is called *Neue und Curieuse Theatralische Tantz-Schule* and is by the dancing-master Gregorio Lambranzi, a Venetian. Nothing whatever seems to be known of this genius. The book consists of a series of engravings by J. G. Puschner, presumably after the drawings by Lambranzi, above each plate is the music of each dance, and at the beginning of the book there are descriptions of every dance in German and Italian. The book was published at Nuremburg in 1716. Harlequin makes frequent appearance, and for sheer poetry and imagination it is impossible to conceive of anything more inspiring than the dances shown here. Every character in comedy is seen in the fullest and most copious variations upon their different *rôles*, and no one who turns over the leaves of this book can fail to recognise in it the supreme monument and culmination of the art of dancing.

[1] Marcellus Laroon the younger (1679-1772), an English artist of Dutch parentage, should be mentioned here. He was a soldier, an adventurer, and at one time a Harlequin in Rich's company. He painted many interiors for the Duke of Montagu, lived to be nearly one hundred years old, and drew most of the large sepia drawings, that are his most familiar work, when about ninety years of age. As a painter he is not much below Cornelius van Troost

My other criterion of this excellence is a set of tapestries to be seen in the Prince Bishop's Palace at Würzburg, in Franconia. After the amazing staircase-ceiling of Tiepolo and the Kaiser-Saal, the hall where the Roman emperors held audience on their way to the coronation at Frankfurt, where Tiepolo painted the ceiling with the crowning and the marriage of Barbarossa, this set of tapestry continues the Italian aspiration, or, if we like, the Cæsarian affectation, of the Holy Roman Empire with a most astounding break into poetry. The tapestries were designed by a Frenchman, Pirot, and were executed, presumably in some German workshop, about the year 1760. They are three in number, and all the characters of Italian comedy figure in them. In one of the tapestries they are eating their supper, and dishes are piled up upon a sideboard in the fashion of those at Veronese's banquets. In another they are playing upon a barge which is floating somewhere on the lagoons of Venice, because in the distance you can see the Piazza and the domes of St. Mark's. In all three of them there are Harlequins, and the artist who conceived them makes the fullest possible use of their chequered clothes, though even in the familiarity of the comedians' supper—for they are feasting seriously and not in character—Harlequin has a menial position and is carrying dishes of food or crossing the foreground to fetch something for the soubrette.

These are instances in which we find the actors of the Italian comedy raised by an artist into the importance of classical gods and goddesses or the saints of Christianity, and the three tapestries invest them with all the attributes of entirely fabulous beings, as though love and money, the two lodestones of life, were in their power and at their command. They have the idyllic conveniences of poetry with a much more substantial furnishing than can be got from a merely wordy wardrobe.

After this paradise of the actor's mind Harlequin is, we must confess, left to himself for some little stay of time. He appears again in the time of Cruikshank when the inimitable Grimaldi had given a new direction to the English harlequinade that Rich had evolved, and when Harlequins, therefore, had taken on a new tenure and shade of life. Hard blows and bruising acrobatics were the material of this school; they were responsible indeed for Grimaldi's tragical retirement long before he was an old man in years. Cruikshank in his early days had much to do with the theatre. It is said that he worked for the juvenile drama of which there are at least two isolated survivals [1] to our day, and he is rumoured to have designed scenery for some of the pantomimes or burlesques of his time. In any case Harlequin comes into many of his drawings, and we emerge straight out of that world of clowns and armoured knights, out of the ranting drama of that day, into the deepest and most sympathetic renderings that Harlequin has ever experienced at the painter's hands.

The greatest of all French artists painted him twice, and conferred by this a double immortality upon what we can only consider as an expiring and perfunctory shade. Once he appears alone, and once in the " Mardi-gras " with a Pierrot, but a Pierrot very different from that of the weekly papers. In the first picture mentioned he is capering quickly across the curiously dead and empty air of the background, which we can only imagine lies waiting for the gaslight. His face appears immobile and masked by his swift step, for Cézanne with unremitting toil had built up a whole durable instant out of his movement. In the second picture he and Pierrot are on their way to the *fête ;* they are hurrying across the picture, drawn along, we have no doubt, by the bands playing in the distance round a few street corners. These two comedians would seem to be amateurs, they have the air of local tradesmen on their way to the Carnival, where they appear every year, perhaps, but only then, in these *rôles*. For Harlequin's final and most complete presentment we must travel a little further.

We arrive at it, about twenty years ago, with the appearance in Paris from Barcelona of Pablo Picasso, the genius in painting of this particular age. All through his career he has painted Harlequins, and in those early stages known as his " blue " and " rose "

---

[1] I refer to Mr. Pollock at Hoxton, and Mr. H. J. Webb at St. Luke's.

periods he must have completed some dozens of these subjects. They must have been one of the strong impressions of his childhood, and in his early pictures on this theme we are reminded of the straight suburbs of Barcelona and the rows of actors' booths, each complete with clown, prostitute, and Harlequin. We can hear the drum-taps and the bugles blown at those canvas doors, and may imagine the sudden codas of Spanish dance stamped and castanetted through these other gaunt invitations. We can remember one particular picture of his with two child-Harlequins, brothers of fifteen and twelve, perhaps, painted against a conventional photographer's backcloth of painted flower-vase and dimly hinted parterre, where these two wasted children show all the inherited taints of camp life, in fact, every hardship of war except the actual bloodshed. They are thin, rickety, with sullen mouths, and the kind of smouldering petulance and inferiority that we can only expect from the offspring of parents who are drinking all the time, and from hours of work that only begin about midnight. In other pictures of his we have Harlequin waiting on a chair just before his cue, or sitting in a café until his time comes.

The great master of concrete and abstract poetry has often painted Harlequin in a kind of abstraction or dilution of guitar music, café tables with the newspapers and glasses laid there, and the mock-sunlight of electricity. He has drawn him, in the other direction, with the patience of Ingres in the most exquisite pencil drawings, save those of Ingres, that have ever been drawn ; but his finest piece of work in this direction, and indeed in many ways the masterpiece of painting of our century, is his curtain for the Russian ballet *Parade*. This shows a whole company of actors at a fair having their supper in the scenery just before the performance. To the usual masks of comedy Picasso has added four more : an American negro boxer, a man and a girl from the films of Texas and the West, and a Spanish guitarist. Needless to say that Harlequin is there in certainly the truest atmosphere ever invented for him by a painter.

Just to finish this documentation before I come to my final

sentences, let me add that one other modern painter has treated Harlequin with energy and attention. This is the Italian—one-time Futurist—Gino Severini, who has evolved a whole series of harlequinades in gouache, or in tempera upon canvas, and who possesses his special theories upon our hero, that he has treated in the most complete fashion in some frescoes in an Italian castle.

I hope that I have now given a tolerably full account of what perpetuity Harlequin has received by means of art. There are, of course, other branches that I have not touched upon : porcelain figures or groups, engravings upon mirrors, or garden statues, in all three of which provinces it would be easy to collect a whole mass of instances. But my avidity has been quashed in thinking of his melancholy history, and so I put aside the hobby of collecting for a few moments' thought about his fate.

The theatrical heroes of every generation seem to die a melancholy death at the hands of the next. Harlequin, one of the longest-lived of them all, has now disappeared even from the Christmas harlequinade at the pantomime, and is only to be found in the suburbs of Barcelona, or on the most distant shores of the Commercial Age. A generation after him have perished in misery and neglect, as we can realise when we think of Dan Leno, George Formby, T. E. Dunville, and Mark Sheridan. In fact, of that whole generation there is only Little Tich still playing to large audiences.

Our hero died in the Harlequin pantomimes that survived till the 'sixties and 'seventies, when we can find, during the half-century this particular kind of production was alive, such titles advertised for Drury Lane, or Covent Garden, as *Harlequin Fat and Harlequin Bat, or, The Giant's Causeway ; Harlequin and Old Gammer Gurtch, or, The Lost Needle ; Harlequin and Jack Frost, or, Old Good Hearty ; Harlequin Hudibras ; Harlequin Sindbad the Sailor, or, The Great Rock of the Diamond Valley and the Seven Wonders of the World ;* and other even more extravagant divagations of the Christmas fancy. Unfortunately for Harlequin, this plenitude of titles meant poor pay and a good many knocks and

xvii

bruises from the rough humour that the gallery expected, and we take leave of him in a crowd of pantomime masks against a fairy transformation of rich tinsel with the Vokes family twisting their long legs and a domestic " drop " for Dan Leno, whom I can just remember, and from whom I may consider I received my introduction into this world of deception.

I must leave my friend, Mr. Beaumont, to give the true facts and manner of Harlequin's history. I have never been able to walk past 75, Charing Cross Road, without pausing, whether the rigours of climate be those of winter or summer, for a few moments' talk with some one who appreciates, as very few do, the glamours and the sequin successes of the stage. His part of the book has been, I know, a labour of love and the fruit of long and protracted investigation. There are dead voices speaking in its pages : we can hear a whole tribe of earlier Harlequins, who with Domenico, and following upon his defect of voice, speak through their throats, giving a peculiar parroty note to their jokes ; Thomassin and Carlin we transport, also, on to this barge on the Venetian lagoons that we have identified in tapestry as the truest background for their art. On other barges forming a regular flotilla we place Harlequin's friends and companions ; there is room, as I have hinted, for Grimaldi and Dan Leno and we will remain there happily floating upon the gentle waves of music until the American clatter and banality have subsided.

SACHEVERELL SITWELL.

26th July, 1926.

Foreword

IN 1922, I contributed to the *Dancing Times* an article on the history of Harlequin, which, as a result of continuous research since that period, has grown into the present volume.

Harlequin is a fascinating subject, but so complicated and well nigh inexhaustible that to deal adequately with his long and tangled history would require the study of a lifetime. This volume therefore is to be regarded simply as a brief summary of the chief events in his career.

I desire to express my gratitude to Mr. Sacheverell Sitwell for having honoured my book with his admirable prologue. I am also indebted for kindly assistance—in the matter of scenery—to Mr. M. Willson Disher, who permitted me to reproduce from his fine collection the two engravings of Carlo Bertinazzi (facing p. 58); to Monsieur Maurice Leloir, who placed at my disposal a photograph and drawings of the costume and mask of an 18th century Italian Harlequin (facing pp. 48 and 60) in his possession; and to Mr. H. J. Webb, who afforded me the same courtesy in regard to the prints of Honor, Ellar and Howard (facing pp. 92, 94 and 96) which form part of his treasury of Theatrical Scenes and Characters for the Juvenile Drama.

CYRIL W. BEAUMONT.

Contents

Illustrations

ILLUSTRATIONS

THE HISTORY OF HARLEQUIN

Chapter One

The Origin of the " Commedia dell' Arte "

" POOR Pierrot ! " The butt of fools, the sport of bullies, the vanquished in love—he has aroused sympathy from his first birthday. His pale, woebegone countenance, his listless air, the long, drooping sleeves of his jacket, everything about him incites pity. But soon it is like to be " Poor Harlequin ! "

His fate is a tragedy greater still. Always merry, radiating the spirit of wit and comedy, and in his movements gay and capricious as a butterfly, he has worn his years lightly. A stranger to sorrow, he feels with added bitterness the neglect that has befallen him in his old age, for daily he trembles between flickering life and extinction. His career resembles that of an ornament passed out of fashion, first set in triumph in the centre of the drawing-room mantelpiece, then moved gradually from room to room as its attraction grows less and less until it is lodged in the attic to await one further and final phase—the dust-bin.

The pedigree of Harlequin resembles an ancient tree with long, straggling roots and many branches intertwined. It is perfectly clear that our English Harlequin is derived from the *Arlecchino* of the Italian Improvised Comedy. But there is no definite evidence to support the theory advocated by some writers that the *Arlecchino* of Italian comedy is a direct descendant from the mimes of ancient Rome. It has been established that the early Romans, like the later Italians, possessed both written comedy and improvised

25

comedy. The former was the entertainment of the educated classes, the latter the amusement of the peasants and common people.

The Roman Improvised Comedy included several denominations of masked buffoons, variously termed *Sanniones*, *Planipedes*, *Stupidi*, etc. The ancient mime Bucco, whose character was that of an acrobatic stupid, has certainly something in common with the early conception of *Arlecchino*. Certain writers have sought to explain that Zanni, the name given to the type of valet, the earliest and most popular of all the Masks, is derived from the Roman buffoon called Sannio. But J. A. Symonds suggests the more acceptable explanation that Zanni " is probably derived from the Bergamasque name for a varlet—Jack ; Zanni being a contraction of Giovanni." The same writer adds : " Nothing could be more uncritical than to assume that the Italian Masks of the sixteenth century A.D. boasted an uninterrupted descent from the Roman Masks of the fifth century B.C. That assumption closes our eyes to a far more interesting aspect of the phenomenon. The fact seems to be that ancient and modern Italy possessed the same mimetic faculty and used it in the same fashion." [1] Dr. Winifred Smith states that, " even admitting the unproved hypothesis that the *Atellanæ* were farces marked by improvisation and masked personages, it would be impossible to establish between them and the Italian extempore plays a connection worthy of the name." [2] Giulio Caprin [3] ridicules the theory that the Italian Masks are directly descended from the buffoons of Roman Improvised Comedy. And Dr. Michele Scherillo prefaces his monograph [4] on the *Commedia dell' Arte* with the significant words " We do not know, nor is it easy to ascertain, the time when this comedy was born."

What then was the origin of the *Commedia dell' Arte* (or to give

[1] Introduction (Part II.) to *The Memoirs of Count Carlo Gozzi*. Trs. by J. A. Symonds. 2 Vols. 1890. Vol. I., p. 38.
[2] *The Commedia dell' Arte*, 1912, pp. 25, 26.
[3] *Carlo Goldoni : la sua vita—le sue opere*. Milano. 1907.
[4] *La Commedia dell' Arte in Italia*. Torino. 1884, p. vii.

COMICO

Io uo uendendo altrui frottole, e fole
rur non contratto mài senza bolletta,
E per più far la mercantia perfetta,
Accresco il capital di capriole.

MORTE

Dal Tarlo mio tu per sottrarti, i salti
Inuan di tua comedia usi, ò faceto
E salti inuan, ch'io farti far decreto
Nella Tragedia mia salti Mortali.

G.o Mitelli F

ARLECCHINO

From the engraving by Giuseppe Maria Mitelli (1634–1718)

its full title, *Commedia dell' Arte all' Improviso*[1]) or Improvised Comedy ? The first attempts at national Italian comedy were the *Cassaria* of Ariosto and the *Calandra* of Bibbiena. The first was produced at Ferrara in 1508, the second at Urbino in 1513. These were followed by the plays of Aretino, Cecchi, Macchiavelli, etc. About 1550, the literary impulse of the Renaissance began to wane, and there arose a new interest in popular forms of art and literature. The highly artificial and precious literature of the Renaissance gave place to a healthy realism, and writers turned to the study of provincial dialects and the life of the peasants. An important playwright of this period is Angelo Beolco, known on the stage as *Il Ruzzante*, or the Frolic, who wrote his first play in 1528 ; in this each character spoke a different dialect.

Plays became simpler in theme, broader in treatment. Presently tumblers, buffoons and their kindred increasingly claimed the popular attention. This variegated and miscellaneous material mingled, jostled and combined, like the pieces of glass in a kaleidoscope, to form a new and definite form of entertainment to be known as the Improvised Comedy.

It has been amply proved that about 1560 the *Commedia dell' Arte* was established in all its main essentials. Probably at first a few people—mountebanks, acrobats and comic actors—formed themselves into a company and set up a simple stage or enclosure at the larger booths and fairs, where they presented an elementary form of play, during the action of which they improvised jokes on the physical peculiarities of certain of the members of their audience and amusing allusions to the local surroundings and traditions. And since reward was in direct proportion to the entertainment afforded, every effort was made to ensure the public's being amused. The whilom acrobat learned to deliver his lines, to " gag." He studied how to emphasise a point by a gesture and by a subtle inflection of the voice, and how to mime. Presently he became an actor of known value and ability who pleased as much

[1] It is also called *Commedia a soggetto, Commedia non scritta, Commedia improvisa.*

by his antics as by his histrionic powers. When these vagrant companies of the fairs took to the theatres, writers of wit and education bent their talents to the service of the new art. They invented new *scenari* and new *lazzi* which increased the company's powers of attraction.

" We give the name of *lazzi*," Riccoboni [1] says, " to those sallies and bits of by-play with which Harlequin and the other Masks interrupt a scene in progress—it may be by demonstration of astonishment or fright, or by humorous extravagances alien to the matter in hand—after which, however, the action has to be renewed on its previous lines." According to the same writer, *lazzi* is the Lombardic pronunciation of the word *lacci*, meaning ribbon. *Lazzi*, therefore, is the means employed by the actor to sustain the action when it tends to drag ; to hold the attention of the audience in expectation of some startling event, or when something important is supposed to be happening behind the scenes ; and to supply a commentary on the words spoken and the gestures made by another ; and to link one scene to the next.

For example, in *Il Convitato di Pietra*, an improvised comedy based on the theme of Don Giovanni, Harlequin, in the presence of Don Giovanni and the Statue, prepares to drink the health of one of his master's favourites. Don Giovanni whispers to him the name of Donna Anna. Harlequin fills his glass, raises it and gives the toast. The Statue bends its head in answer. Harlequin, terror-stricken, turns a somersault with the full glass in his hand. In another play, Harlequin, while his masters discuss serious matters, pretends to catch a fly, pull off its wings and eat the body. In another piece Harlequin pretends to have his hat full of cherries, which he eats, throwing the stones at his fellow-actors.

Apart from the *lazzi*, each actor had his *Repertorio*, or collection of polite and impolite phrases, exclamations, oaths and so forth, which he drew upon as occasion demanded. The lover had his *concetti*, containing his store of high-flown compliments, bursts of eloquence, and ravings with which he laid siege to the heart of

[1] *Histoire du Théâtre Italien*, 1728, p. 65.

FIGURES OF THE "COMMEDIA DELL' ARTE"

From the tapestry designed by A. Pirot in the Schloss at Würzburg

his lady. The father had his admonitory speeches to his son. The captain had his *bravure*, which consisted of bragging boasts and terrifying threats. The doctor had his *tirata della giostra*, a ridiculous farrago of long-winded explanations interlarded with sonorous Latin phrases with which he argued a legal point. But when the actor was an artist, he improved on the traditional sayings, giving them a new turn and adding quips of his own invention which combined to afford a new conception of the part.

"To be a good Italian actor," says Gherardi,[1] " means to be a man who possesses a rich store of knowledge ; who plays more from fancy than from memory ; who, while he plays, invents all he says ; who seconds his colleagues on the stage, that is, matches his words and actions so well with those of his comrade that he enters at once in all the movements to which the other invites him, and in such a way as to make everybody believe that all has been prearranged."

The plots were invariably stories of amorous intrigue. They were generally concerned with two young people in love with one another, the parents or guardians employing all kinds of devices to prevent the lovers meeting, while the servants used the most complicated stratagems to aid the lovers. The performance reflected the dissolute character of the age. In the vital necessity of keeping the audience amused, there were few scruples at the introduction of obscenity. Unpleasant vices were discussed in the most liberal and open manner ; episodes of shipwreck and fire were taken full advantage of for presenting a man or woman half naked or in torn and transparent clothes ; there were many scenes in which a man sought concealment beneath a woman's skirts ; and Otonelli writes that on one occasion in 1635, when he went to a theatre, " there was an actor who, in order to call forth roars of laughter, made a gesture of such unsurpassed indecency that all, even the most light-minded, were so ashamed that they drooped their eyes." [2] The early *Commedia dell' Arte* was a hotch-potch of

[1] *Le Théâtre Italien*, 6 Vols., 1717. Vol. I., p. iii.
[2] *Della Christiana Moderatione del Theatro*, 1646. Quoted by Mantzius. *A History of Theatrical Art*. Trs. by L. von Cossel. 6 Vols., 1903–21. Vol. II., p. 230.

excellent parody, adroit wit and caustic satire mingled with acrobatics and buffoonery of the most elemental and obscene order.
It must be stated, however, that the moral tone of the impromptu
comedy of the seventeenth and eighteenth centuries showed some
improvement.

It is difficult to ascertain exactly what was meant by the term
Commedia dell' Arte. Some authorities hold that *arte* implied a
craft or guild to explain that the performances were given by
professional actors. Others assert that *arte* meant craft in another
sense, that the actors were artisans, like the players who perform
Pyramus and Thisbe in Shakespeare's *A Midsummer Night's
Dream*. The main fact is that the *Commedia dell' Arte*, or Improvised Comedy, was for the most part the transitory creation of the
actor who played it, the performance being improvised from a brief
outline of the plot pinned up behind the scenes to which the actor
referred during the progress of the play. Prior to the performance
the plot was discussed, the manner of presentation arranged, the
characters distributed, the entrances and exits fixed, and the main
details of the " business " worked out. It should not be forgotten
that the improvisation was only partial, since each player possessed
a fund of stock phrases, or *Repertorio*, which has been described ;
and it was rare for an actor to devote his studies to more than one
type of character.

In connection with the preparation of a play it is of interest to
quote the words of Perrucci, a seventeenth century writer on the
technique of the *Commedia dell' Arte*, regarding the duties of the
Capocomico or *Choregus*, the director of the company, who was
usually the principal actor or manager of the troupe :—

The *Choregus*, who rules and guides the troupe by his ability and experience, has to plan the subject, to show how the action shall be conducted, the
dialogues concluded, and new sallies of wit and humour introduced. It is
not merely his business to read the plot aloud, but also to set forth the
personages, with their names and qualities, to explain the drama, describe
localities, and suggest extemporaneous additions. For instance, he shall
begin by saying : " The comedy we have to present is so-and-so, the
personages such-and-such ; the houses are on this side and on that."

30

FIGURES OF THE " COMMEDIA DELL' ARTE "

From the tapestry designed by A. Pirot in the Schloss at Würzburg

Then he will unfold the argument. He will impress upon his comrades the necessity of bearing well in mind the place where they are supposed to be, the names of people and the business they are engaged in, so that they shall not confound Rome with Naples, or say that they have come from Spain when they are bound from Germany. A father must not forget his son's name, nor a lover his lady's. It is also most important that the houses in which the action has to take place should be accurately known. To knock at the wrong door, or to take refuge in the home of your enemy, would spoil all. Afterwards the planner of the subject must indicate occasions suited to the sallies of the several characters.

" Here a piece of buffoonery is right. A metaphor, or sarcasm, or hyperbole, or innuendo, would make a good effect there." In fact, he has to show each actor how to play his part to best advantage in the circumstances of the piece. Then he must look to preventing inconvenient entrances and exits, providing that the stage be not left empty, and indicating proper ways of bringing scenes to their conclusion. After the *Choregus* has read this lecture to the troupe, they will meet and sketch the comedy in outline. Then they have the opportunity of bringing their own talents forward and combining new effects. Yet, at such rehearsals, they must all be mindful to maintain the outlines of the subject, not to exceed their *rôles*, nor yet to trust their recollection of similar plays performed under different conditions. The piece has each time to be produced afresh by the concerted action of the players who will bring it on the boards.[1]

[1] Perucci (A.), *Dell' Arte Rappresentativa premeditata ed all' improviso*, 1699. Quoted Symonds, *Op. cit.*, Vol. I., p. 58.

Chapter Two

The Principal Companies of the Italian Comedians in the Sixteenth Century

THE *Commedia dell' Arte* dates, as we have noted, from the latter half of the sixteenth century. The troupes increased in number and journeyed far and wide. They appeared in France, England, Austria, Bavaria, Portugal and Spain. It would appear that the actors learned their business at home and traded it to greater advantage abroad. Since, in the course of this volume, it will be necessary to make frequent reference to these various troupes, it is advisable to review briefly the travels of the principal companies.

Italian comedians of some kind visited France as early as 1530, but it is not until 1548 that there is mention of an Italian company which gave a remarkable performance of Bibbiena's *Calandra* at Lyon, during the festivities held in honour of the triumphal entry into that town of Henry III. and his Queen, Catherine de Medici.

In 1571, an important company styled *I Comici Confidenti*, or The Confident Comedians, well-known throughout Italy, entered France and journeyed through the provinces, giving performances of impromptu comedies, pastorals and written comedies.

The *Confidenti* were followed almost concurrently by another company, directed by Alberto Ganassa.[1] They had played in

---

[1] Also written *Ganesse, Gavasse, Gavazza, Gavazzi.*

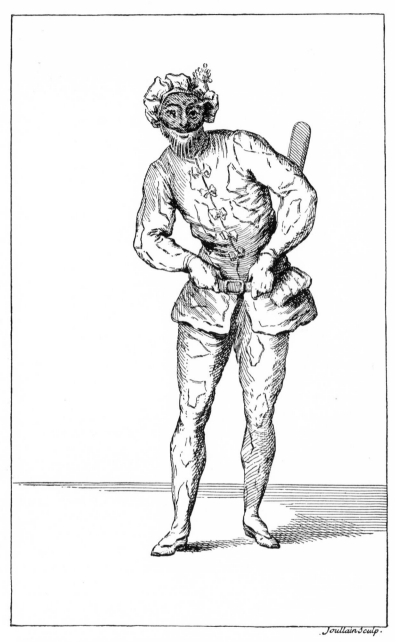

Joullain Sculp.

ITALIAN HARLEQUIN, MIDDLE OF THE 16TH CENTURY

*From the Etching by Joullain in Riccoboni's " Histoire de l'Ancien
Théâtre Italien," 1728*

Spain during 1565, giving farces in Italian which were received with great applause. They were at Mantua in 1568, at Milan in 1569 and at Ferrara in 1570.

It would appear that they visited Paris early in the following year, for Lord Buckhurst—the special ambassador sent by Queen Elizabeth to congratulate Charles IX. on his marriage—who arrived there on the 15th of February, writing to his sovereign on the 4th of March, 1571, describes a performance by the Italian comedians, possibly the first occasion on which the *Commedia dell' Arte* had been seen in the capital : " The 4 of this month the King procures the duke de Nevers to invite me to diner where we found a sumptuous feste and of gret honour adorned w^t musick of a most excellent and straunge conserte, and w^t a Comedie of Italians that for the good mirth and handling therof deserved singular commendacion." [1]

On the 1st of May, Ganassa's company played at Nogent-le-Roy on the occasion of a royal baptism. It is difficult to trace their subsequent movements, but it is certain that they were in Paris in September, because the *Parlement* issued a decree dated 15th September prohibiting all public performances by " players of farces and such like common amusements " [2] who were not properly authorised. The troupe were further charged with asking exorbitant prices for admission. The price of the places, fixed at from three to five sols,[3] was regarded as a monstrous imposition on the people. Ganassa showed his permits from the King in which they were styled *Comédiens du Roi*, but to no avail, for, to be valid, these letters patent should have been registered by the *Parlement*. The matter was again discussed in a decree dated the 15th of October, in which the company were referred to more courteously as " Albert Ganasse and his companions," actors of " tragedies and

---

[1] *Calendar of State Papers, Foreign Series of the Reign of Elizabeth*, 1569–1571, p. 413.

[2] See Baschet (A.), *Les Comédiens Italiens*, 1882, pp. 16 *et seq.*, for a detailed account of the troubles with the *Parlement*.

[3] A *sol* or *sou* was originally the twentieth part of a *livre*, and is now the name of the French halfpenny, which is the twentieth part of a *franc*.

comedies." Ganassa did not apparently pursue the matter, and returned to Italy, since there is mention of his company's performing at Milan early in 1572.

They revisited Paris in August of the same year to take part in the festivities held in honour of the marriage of Henry, King of Navarre, with Marguerite de Valois. There exists in the Bayeux Museum an interesting painting on wood by Paul Porbus,[1] executed about 1572, which depicts a masquerade at the Court of Charles IX. and probably represents some of the members of Ganassa's troupe acting with certain of the courtiers. In May, 1574, Charles IX. died, and although there are no details concerning the company, it is not unlikely that they remained in Paris until his death. In this same year Ganassa went to Spain, where he revived his former success and amassed considerable wealth.

Then there were the troupes of Antonio Maria, of Venice, and Soldini, of Florence, consisting of nine and eleven actors respectively. Both these companies were in the employ of Charles IX. from February, 1572, and appear to have acted together at Paris and Blois according to the King's pleasure. The Earl of Lincoln, the special ambassador to Queen Elizabeth, in a letter from the Louvre dated the 18th of June, 1572, possibly describes a performance by the Maria-Soldini company : "At aftar dynar Monsr and his brother browght us to a chambre wheare was vearie many sorts of exelent musicke ; and after that, he had us to another large chambre wheare there was an Italian playe, and dyvars vantars and leapers of dyvars sortes, vearie exelent ; and thus that daie was spent."[2] These companies were to have taken part in the celebrations held in honour of the marriage of Henry of Navarre with Marguerite de Valois ; but, owing to the death of Jeanne d'Albret, the festivities were postponed to the 18th of August, and so the players departed.

[1] A reproduction of this painting will be found in Duchartre (P. L.), *La Comédie Italienne*, Nouv. Edit., 1925, p. 77.

[2] Nichols (J.), *Progresses and Public Processions of Queen Elizabeth*, 3 Vols., 1823. Vol. I., p. 304.

ITALIAN HARLEQUIN (1570)

From Sand's "Masques et Buffons"

From 1560 to 1575, dramatic art in Italy flourished exceedingly. It was in high favour with the people, enjoyed the patronage of many wealthy nobles, and its actors were excellent. Some members of Ganassa's company did not follow him to Spain but went to Venice, where they were reformed and directed by Flaminio Scala, who played the lover's *rôle* of *Flavio*. The company took the title of *I Comici Gelosi*, or The Jealous Comedians, and played throughout Italy, visiting Venice, Rome, Naples, Milan, Bologna, Mantua, Ferrara and Turin, according to the season of the year. There is mention of their performing before the Emperor of Austria in 1576.

It was in July, 1574, at Venice, that Henry III. saw this troupe on his return from Poland to France to succeed to the throne left vacant by the death of Charles IX. The Venetian republic, well disposed towards France, held splendid festivities in honour of the new monarch. The King having expressed his eagerness to witness the Italian comedians, the *Gelosi*, then at Milan, were requested to hasten with all despatch to Venice to take part in the celebrations. The company included Francesco Andreini as *Capitano Spavento*, Simone of Bologna as *Harlequin*, Giulio Pasquati as *Pantalone*, and the famous Vittoria as *Fioretta*. The King was delighted, particularly with the " *divina* Vittoria."

He left Venice on the 27th of July and arrived at Lyon the 6th of September. From this time until 1576 he was fully occupied with the Huguenots. The strain of state affairs beginning to weigh heavily upon him, he sought relief in amusements. He had not forgotten the *Gelosi*, and on the 25th of May he wrote to M. du Ferrier, his ambassador at Venice, to seek out the *Gelosi* and invite them to France, and provide them with the necessary money for their journey.[1]

In 1574, the *Confidenti* and the *Gelosi* combined under the title of *I Comici Uniti*, or The United Comedians, but towards the end of the year 1576 the companies separated, Flaminio Scala continuing to be the director of the *Gelosi*. It was possibly due to

[1] See Baschet, *op. cit.*, p. 63, for a transcription of the letter.

35

these changes that the company did not set out so quickly for France as the King desired, for they did not arrive at Blois until the 25th of January, 1577. Their journey, too, had not been free from difficulties, for on their way from Lyon to Blois they were captured by Huguenots at La Charité-sur-Loire and the King was forced to pay their ransom. The diligent L'Estoile notes thus in his journal their arrival :

> In this month (February) the Italian comedians styled *I Gelosi* whom the King had sent for from Venice, expressly for his diversion, and whose ransom he had paid, they having been captured and plundered by Huguenots, about last Christmas-tide, began to perform their comedies in the Salle des Etats at Blois ; and the King permitted them to charge a half testoon[1] to all who should come to see them play.[2]

The King left for Amboise on the 23rd of April, while the *Gelosi* went to seek their fortunes in Paris. L'Estoile records that :

> On Sunday, the 19th of May, the Italian comedians, surnamed *I Gelosi*, began the performance of their Italian comedies at the Hôtel de Bourbon, in Paris ; they charged a fee of four sols per head to all the French who wished to see them act, and such were the crowds they attracted that the four best preachers of Paris had not amongst them all as many present when they discoursed.[3]

But the *Parlement*, doubtless at the instigation of the *Confrérie de la Passion*,[4] which owned the dramatic monopoly in Paris, put an end to their performances, since they were of the opinion that their plays taught only " *paillardise et adultères* " and served as " a school of debauchery to the youth of both sexes in the city of Paris."

---

[1] A *teston* (testoon), so called from the head on its obverse, was worth about ten *sols*.

[2] *Mémoires-Journaux de Pierre de l'Estoile.* 12 Vols. 1875. Vol. I., p. 179.

[3] *Id.*, Vol. I., p. 189.

[4] All theatrical business in Paris was controlled by a dramatic society of artisans known as the *Confrérie de la Passion*, which, by virtue of a royal privilege granted in 1402, had the sole right to prohibit all theatrical performances of which they did not reap the profits. The original privilege was confirmed by all the successive Kings until 1677.

GIOVANNI BATTISTA ANDREINI

From Andreini's " L'Adamo," 1613

The *Gelosi* again presented the King's letters, this time with better results, since they were presently backed by an order from the King to the city authorities in which he commanded them to permit the *Gelosi* to give their performances. The note is curt and to the point : " I desire that it be done so and that there shall be no mistake, for I have pleasure in hearing them and have never heard more perfect." [1] L'Estoile states that :

On the 27th of July the Italian comedians, *I Gelosi*, after having presented at Court letters patent granted them by the King, permitting them to perform their Comedies, notwithstanding the prohibition of the Court, were dismissed under plea of objection with prohibition ever to obtain and to present such letters to the Court subject to a penalty of ten thousand livres, [2] to be paid into the poor-box. Notwithstanding this inhibition, in the early part of the following September they renewed the performance of their comedies at the Hôtel de Bourbon as before, by the King's express command ; the corruption of these times being such that comedians, buffoons, harlots and mignons enjoy the fullest credit with the King. [3]

The *Gelosi* returned to Florence in 1578, when F. Andreini succeeded F. Scala as director, and the troupe was reformed to include the finest talent available. The company contained Ludovico of Bologna, as Harlequin : Francesco Andreini, as Captain Spavento : and the director's wife, the beautiful and famous Isabella.

In 1583, another company of Italian comedians under the direction of Battista Lazzaro came to Paris. They played not at the Hôtel de Bourbon but at the Hôtel de Bourgogne, which was rented to them for a *demi-écu* [4] weekly. But the director having failed to keep his engagements, the company were driven out and their property seized.

---

[1] See Baschet, *op. cit.*, p. 76.

[2] The *livre*, which originally was the weight of a lb. of silver, became the equivalent of 20 *sols*. After 1667, the *livre tournois* was the only one recognised.

[3] *Op. cit.*, Vol. I., p. 202.

[4] At first the *écu* (crown) was a gold coin and its value altered from 18 *sols* to 4 *livres*, 24 *sols*. Louis XIII. and XIV. struck silver *écus* having a value of 60 *sols*, but this varied almost with each emission.

The *Confidenti* revisited Paris in 1584 and remained there for one year until expelled by the *Confrérie de la Passion*.

In 1599, the *Gelosi* would seem to have again returned to Paris. They were, of course, free to perform at Court but, when they sought to give public performances at the Hôtel de Bourgogne, the *Confrérie de la Passion* prevented them from doing so. A few days later, however, a permit was granted them to play, possibly because the company paid a considerable sum of money in consideration of the privilege.

ITALIAN HARLEQUIN (1671)

From Sand's " Masques et Buffons "

Chapter Three

*The Principal Companies of the Italian Comedians in the
Seventeenth Century*

A TROUPE known as the *Accesi*, or Duke of Mantua's Company, directed by Tristano Martinelli, who played the Mask of Harlequin, arrived at Lyon in August, 1600. They travelled to Paris, where they remained until October, 1601, when the company went back to Italy. Ten years later the *Accesi* again visited France, returning to Italy.

On the 26th of August, 1613, the company played at Lyon and then went to Paris, where they remained until September, when they passed to Fontainebleau. Shortly afterwards, they again took the road to Paris, where they played sometimes at the Hôtel de Bourgogne for the public and sometimes at the Louvre for the pleasure of the Court.

It is not until 1621 that there is again mention of the *Accesi*, when it is recorded that they played at Paris, at the Hôtel de Bourbon, and at Fontainebleau.

In 1600, the *Gelosi* were called to Paris by Henry IV. on the occasion of his marriage with Marie de Medici. This company played there until 1604. In this same year Isabella Andreini died at Lyon while travelling to Italy, and her husband dispersed the company and retired to devote himself to preparing his wife's works for publication.[1]

[1] Andreini (I.), *Lettere della Signore Isabella Andreini, Padovana Comica gelosa*

In 1605, the *Gelosi* were re-established by Giovanni Battista Andreini, the son of Isabella, under the new title of *I Comici Fedeli*, or The Faithful Comedians. Andreini played the Mask of Harlequin and also the lover's part of *Lelio*. This troupe came to Paris in 1613 at the request of Marie de Medici, and played at the Hôtel de Bourgogne, on alternate days with the French comedians. They also gave performances at the Louvre. From 1618 to 1621, the company traversed Italy and then returned to Paris, where they remained until 1623. The troupe revisited Paris in 1624 and remained there until early in 1625.

The *Confidenti* were at Lucques in 1616, and at Venice in 1618.

In 1639, Louis XIII. summoned from Italy the company directed by Giuseppe Bianchi, which performed operas and improvised comedies. This troupe included Tiberio Fiorilli, the celebrated Scaramouch. The Harlequin was Domenico Locatelli. The company left in 1648, owing to the troubles of the Fronde.

Five years later another company appeared in Paris, probably jointly directed by Fiorilli and Locatelli; it contained many of the players of Bianchi's troupe. They were the first to settle definitely in Paris. The performances were given at the Petit Bourbon Theatre. In 1659, the company was further enlarged by several excellent players summoned from Italy by Cardinal Mazarin. These were Domenico Biancolelli, to be world famous as Harlequin; Orsola Cortesi (*Eularia*); Patrizia Adami (*Diamantina*), and Giovanni Andrea Zanotti (*Ottavio*).

In 1660, the company moved to the theatre of the Palais Royal, which they shared with Molière's troupe, performances being given on alternate days. In 1684, the actors began to depart from their fixed practice of playing their comedies in Italian, so that French words began to be introduced into the dialogue. This innovation led to the interpolation of whole scenes in the latter language. Domenico died on the 2nd of August, 1688, and the Mask of

et Academica Intenta, nominata l'Accesa. Venetia. 1607.—*Fragmenti di alcune scritture . . . raccolti da F. Andreini, e dati in luce da F. Scala.* Venetia. 1647. —*Le Rime d'Isabella Andreini.* Napoli. 1696.

DEPARTURE OF THE ITALIAN COMEDIANS IN 1697

From the engraving after Antoine Watteau

Harlequin was played by Evaristo Gherardi, who joined the company in October, 1689.

Towards the end of the century, either the plays had become too gross or the Parisians too refined, for a rèference to the Italian players in some contemporary correspondence states that :

> The King, having been informed that the Italians make indecent representations and speak many unpleasantnesses in their plays, His Majesty has forbidden them through M. de la Tremoille neither to make nor say such things in the future . . . and if they should happen to make an indecent gesture or say equivocal words or anything contrary to public decency, His Majesty will suppress them and send them back to Italy.[1]

In 1697, the King's Company of Italian Comedians were suppressed. According to several writers, this was due to their having performed a piece entitled *La Fausse Prude*, in which unwelcome allusions to Madame de Maintenon were made. This is an error. A piece entitled *La Fausse Prude* was never played, the last play given by the company being *Spinette, ou Le Lutin Amoureux*, which was presented in April, 1697. It was chiefly remarkable for the performance by a new actress called Spinetta, who played six different characters in the piece.

La Fausse Prude was the name of a romance published at this time in Holland which, on account of the scandals regarding Madame de Maintenon it was rumoured to disclose, was strictly forbidden to be imported into France. Now the Italian players had put into rehearsal a comedy called *La Belle-Mère Supposée*, which had been given on former occasions in Italian under its original title, *La Finta Matrigna*. Some misguided actors thought it would add to the play's attraction if it were renamed *La Fausse Prude* after the sensational novel ; which suggestion was adopted. This imprudence delivered the players into the hands of their enemies who, one may be sure, carried a fine tale to the King.

Retribution was swift. Before even the play had been given,

---

[1] Quoted Campardon (E.), *Les Comédiens du Roi de la Troupe Italienne*. 2Vols. 1880. Vol. I., p. xxiii.

M. de Pontchartrain wrote on the 13th of May to M. de la Reynie, Lieutenant-General of Police :

> The King has expelled his Italian comedians, and His Majesty commands me to write to you to close their theatre to-morrow for ever.[1]

At eleven o'clock the following morning, M. d'Argenson (who had just succeeded M. de la Reynie as Lieutenant-General of Police), accompanied by numerous commissaries and a body of archers, entered the Hôtel de Bourgogne and affixed seals to the doors of the dressing-rooms and the entrance doors to the theatre.

It is of interest to note the composition of the company at the time of its suppression. It consisted of Angelo Constantini (*Mezzetino*), Giovanni Battista Constantini [2] (*Ottavio*), Michel-Angelo Fracanzani (*Pulcinella*), Evaristo Gherardi (*Harlequin*), Giuseppe Giaratoni (*Pierrot*), Marc' Antonio Romagnesi (*Cinthio*), Carlo Virgili Romagnesi di Belmont (*Leandre*), Giuseppe Tortoriti (*Pasquariello*), Caterina Biancolelli (*Columbine*), Angelica Toscano (*Marinetta*), Spinetta, Elizabeth Daneret (*Babet la Cantatrice*), and the machinist-painter Cadet.

Not long afterwards the King accorded Tortoriti and Cadet permission to form two troupes to be allowed to give performances in the provinces, subject to their not appearing within thirty leagues of Paris. Many of the disbanded comedians joined one or other of these companies.

[1] Jal (A.), *Dictionnaire Critique de Biographie et d'Histoire*. Paris. 1867, p. 410.
[2] Also written *Costantini*.

DANCE BETWEEN HARLEQUIN AND SCARAMOUCH

From Lambranzi's " Neue und Curieuse Theatralische Tantz-Schule," 1716

Chapter Four

The Principal Companies of the Italian Comedians in the Eighteenth Century

IN 1716, the Regent, Philippe, Duc d'Orleans, desirous of reviving the glories of the Italian comedians who had afforded him such entertainment in his youth, instructed Luigi Riccoboni, an actor celebrated under the name of Lelio, to form a company and bring it to France.

Riccoboni chose the best players of the company in the service of Antonio Farnese, Prince of Parma, who, anxious to please both the King of France and the Regent, consented to their departure subject to their playing " with all modesty before His Majesty as well as His Highness the Duc d'Orleans." The same document [1] appointed Riccoboni in charge of his comrades and regulated questions affecting their repertory, costumes, finance, etc., and allowed each actor an equal share in the distribution of profits. The first performance was given at the Palais Royal Theatre on the 18th of May, 1716, in the presence of the Regent and the Duchesse de Berry, the play selected being *L'Inganno Fortunato*. Its success was prodigious, particularly on account of the excellent *lazzi* invented by Thomassin as Harlequin.

The old theatre of the Hôtel de Bourgogne was repaired ; and there, on the 1st of June, the company presented *La Folle Supposée*,

---

[1] This document is printed in full in Campardon, *op. cit.*, Vol. II., p. 231.

a play based on Regnard's *Folies Amoureuses* and Molière's *L'Amour Médecin*. In honour of the reinstallation of the Italian comedians the curtain was painted with the device of a phœnix surrounded by flames, with the legend *Je renais*.

In 1723, Louis XV. accorded a pension of 15,000 livres to Riccoboni's troupe, and on the doors of the Hôtel de Bourgogne, below the arms of France, there was placed a plaque of black marble bearing in letters of gold the inscription :

Hostel des Comédiens ordinaires du Roy, entretenus par Sa Majesté, rétablis à Paris en l'année MDCCXVI.[1]

The representations consisted of singing, dancing, mimed scenes and spoken dialogue and improvisation.

By the middle of the eighteenth century the repertory of the Italian comedians had become extremely varied. It included plays entirely in Italian ; Italian plays interpolated with scenes in French ; parodies ; French comedies, which generally concluded with dances and songs ; and even comedies with which firework displays were combined. This versatility led to constant quarrels with the directors of other theatres, who regarded certain types of entertainment as their own particular property.

In 1726, the Comédie Italienne was amalgamated with the Theatre of the Opéra Comique, which conferred on the former the legal right to sing. But, as we have seen, the want of this privilege had not prevented the Italians from introducing singing into their comedies. Now singing began to encroach more and more on dialogue, once the principal feature of their performances. The taste for Italian plays fast declined, being kept alive only by Carlin's splendid miming. Soon the Comédie Italienne was simply a theatre presenting comic operas or written pieces by French authors, like Anseaume, Boissy, Delisle, Desportes, Favart, Fuselier, Lanoue, Marivaux, Poinsinet, Sedaine, and so on, while the music was provided by Duni, Grétry, Philidor and Monsigny.

From 1763 to 1768 the receipts began steadily to decline. This

[1] Campardon, *op. cit.*, Vol. I., p. xxxiii.

the players attributed to the continued performance of French comedies, which, in their opinion, had become so well known as to have lost their powers of attraction. Accordingly they withdrew all French plays and acted instead Italian pieces and French vaudevilles and operettas. But by 1779 the public had tired of Italian pieces and clamoured for the French plays to be revived. These were again performed and the Italian plays withdrawn. Grimm wrote in April, 1779 :

> The Comédie Italienne having obtained permission not to perform any more Italian pieces, has replaced these by others of its old repertory which it had entirely abandoned after its amalgamation with the Opéra Comique. Consequently all our ultramontane actors have been dismissed with the exception of Carlin Bertinazzi and his double, who continue to perform their part of Harlequin in the French comedies.[1]

On the 25th of December in the same year the State Council issued an order, to take effect from Easter, 1780, declaring the company of Italian comedians suppressed and abolished, and providing for the formation of a new troupe from those actors and actresses already playing in French comedies and operas, who were to retain the same position they occupied in the old company and to play the same characters.

In 1780, the theatre of the Comédie Italienne assumed the name of the Théâtre des Italiens, despite the fact that at that time there was no longer a single Italian actor connected with it.

---

[1] *Correspondance Litteraire, Philosophique et Critique addressée à un Souverain d'Allemagne.* 17 Vols. 1812–14. Part II., Vol. IV., p. 380.

Chapter Five

On the Origin and Costume of Harlequin

THE Masks, or fixed characters, were derived from all the provinces of Italy. The four chief and oldest Masks were *Arlecchino, Brighella, Pantalone* and *Il Dottore*. The first two were natives of Bergamo, the third came from Venice, and the last from Bologna. If the origin of Harlequin (*Arlecchino*) be examined, it will be found that, in common with his relations, he was a type built up on the peculiarities of the residents of a province. An early writer records that the inhabitants of Bergamo could be divided into two entirely opposed types. Those of the upper part of the town were hard-working, lively and quick at repartee ; these were the qualities of Brighella. The residents of the lower part were gluttonous, stupid and lazy ; these were the original characteristics of Harlequin.

What is the etymology of Harlequin ? It is said that one of the principal buffoons of an Italian troupe of comedians that came to Paris in the sixteenth century secured the protection of Achille du Harlay, first president of the *Parlement*. As a result of this good fortune the actor's comrades nicknamed him *Harlayquino*. Another writer states, with more probability, that Harlequin is a diminutive of *harle*, or *herle*, the name given to an aquatic bird, this term being applied in allusion to the sprightly movements of a particular type of buffoon. Harlequin spelt his name in a variety

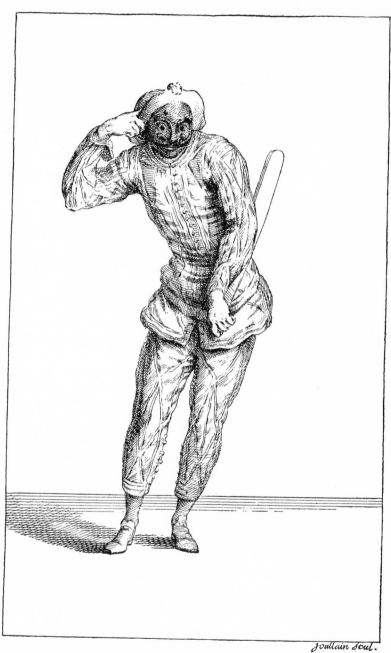

Joullain Scul.

ITALIAN HARLEQUIN, EARLY 18TH CENTURY

*From the Etching by Joullain in Riccoboni's " Histoire de
l'Ancien Théâtre Italien," 1728*

of ways : first, *Harlequinus* and *Herlequinus ;* next, *Harlequino,
Harlechino, Arlechino, Arlichino ;* and latterly *Harlechino* and *Arlec-
chino.* In France he was known as *Hellequin, Herlequin, Herlekin,
Hierlikin, Hielekin, Helquin,* and then *Arlechin* and *Arlequin.* In
England he was called *Harlicken, Harlakene, Harlakeene* and
Harlequin.

What is the costume of Harlequin ? Probably the earliest
illustration of the character is that contained in a little book entitled
Compositions de Rhetorique, written by Martinelli, the Harlequin
of the *Accesi,* called to Paris in 1600 by Henry IV. to take part in
the festivities held on the occasion of his marriage with Marie de
Medici. It was written to remind the King and Queen of their
promise to present him with a gold chain and medal.

This volume contains a few illustrations of Martinelli as
Harlequin. They show the actor dressed like a servant in a jacket
reaching half-way to the knee, and narrow trousers, the whole
covered with irregular patches. His feet are covered with black
shoes ; his waist is girded by a belt which sustains a stout wooden
sword and leather wallet. On his head is a soft cap, apparently
decorated with a hare's or rabbit's scut. The upper part of his
face is concealed by a black half-mask, fringed to suggest a mous-
tache and whiskers, while his chin boasts a short beard (see
Pl. fcg. p. 46).

Riccoboni, in his *Histoire du Théâtre Italien,* also shows an
engraving of an early Harlequin (see Pl. fcg. p. 32). The costume
is similar to that worn by Martinelli, except that the trousers and
jacket are tight-fitting and the latter is tied with ribbons instead of
laces. His feet are encased in light shoes ; his head is covered with
a soft cap, of the type fashionable during the reign of Francis I. or
Henry II., likewise decorated with a hare's or rabbit's scut. The
half-mask is the same, but the chin is almost concealed by bristling
false whiskers.

Writers who favour the connection between the Roman mimes
and the actors of the Italian Improvised Comedy assert that the
patches of Harlequin's costume have their origin in the tigers'

skins worn by the ancient actors who played the part of satyrs. It is far more likely that they are simply the patched garments of a poor country menial.

About the middle of the seventeenth century these patches became a symmetrical pattern of triangles variously coloured blue, red and green, and bordered with a narrow yellow braid. At the same time the " tights " were exchanged for trousers which reached to the ankle ; the bows on the coat were replaced by metal buttons. The legs were covered with white stockings, and the feet with brown shoes decorated with buckles or bows. The head was covered with a black skull cap, over which was worn a grey felt hat, crested with the inevitable hare's scut, which took the place of the former soft cap. The sword was longer, lighter and more graceful (see Pl. fcg. p. 38).

In the eighteenth century the triangles of the costume became lozenges, the tunic was shorter, and the trousers were close-fitting (see Pl. fcg. p. 44).

The mask proper to Harlequin of the later period consists of a black leather half-mask and a chin-piece of the same material and colour (see Pl. fcg. p. 48). The eyebrows are bristling and slightly raised to suggest an air of mild astonishment. A large wart is placed on the forehead above the right eye. Small holes set each side of the nose indicate the eyes. The whole conveys a curious mixture of devilry, mockery, sensuality, artfulness and mystery. The origin of the mask is not clear. Apart from the obvious purpose of accentuating the qualities of the character, we are inclined to think that, since the mask was worn only by the buffoon characters, it was employed as a means of disguise.

The hare's or rabbit's scut was both an emblem of speed and a token of pusillanimity. Goldoni, in his Memoirs, has a reference to this portion of Harlequin's attire which opens up a very interesting question. He writes :

In traversing the country of Harlequin, I was curious to observe whether there was any existing trace of that comic character which afforded such entertainment to the Italian theatre. I could see neither the black visages,

48

PAGES FROM MARTINELLI'S "COMPOSITIONS DE RHETORIQUE,"
1601

From the unique copy in the Bibliothèque Nationale, Paris

nor the small eyes, nor the ludicrous parti-coloured dress, but I observed the hare tails in the hats with which the peasants of those districts are still equipped.[1]

Did Harlequin, derived from the Bergamask peasant, deck his cap with a hare's scut out of respect to tradition, or did the Bergamask peasants wear a hare's scut in honour of Harlequin ?

The purpose of the wooden stick or sword is not known with certainty. It has been likened to the wand or *caduceus* of Mercury, with which the god made himself invisible and caused himself to be transported whither he willed. But although this magical quality is presumed to be resident in the wand or bat which forms part of the equipment of the familiar Harlequin of our pantomimes, it is not clear that the wooden sword of his Italian ancestor was endowed with a similar power.

Maurice Sand[2] sees in the bat of Harlequin a modification of the curved stick of the peasants of the Greek theatre, the attribute of comedy. It seems to us extremely unlikely that the original rough and ready actor of the Mask of Harlequin should have been acquainted with the traditions of the Greek theatre and hence worn or carried a stick on that account. We suggest that it was thrust into his belt because nearly every peasant of that time carried a stick as a companion and a measure of self-defence, while on the stage such a " property " offered countless opportunities as a factor in creating humorous incidents and by-play.

[1] *Memoirs of Goldoni.* Trs. from the original French by John Black. 2 Vols. 1814. Vol. I., p. 177.
[2] *Masques et Buffons.* 2 Vols. 1860. Vol. I., p. 37.

Chapter Six

On the Qualities of Harlequin and some Celebrated Players
of the Character

WHAT was the part of Harlequin ? Riccoboni states that—

Down to the seventeenth century Harlequin's performance consisted simply of a series of extravagant capers, of violent movements and outrageous blackguardisms. He was at once insolent mocking, clownish and, above all, obscene. I think that with all this he mingled an agility of body which made him appear always in the air, and I might add with assurance that he was an acrobat.[1]

So far as can be ascertained, Alberto Ganassa was the first actor to play the Mask of Harlequin, for the Sieur de la Fresnaye Vauquelin says of his appearance in Paris :

> . . . ou le bon Pantalon, ou Zany dont Ganasse
> Nous a representé le façon et la grace. . . .[2]

The next was Simone of Bologna, the original Harlequin of the *Gelosi*. But the first of whom there exists any account was Tristano Martinelli. He was a native of Mantua, and, according to Rasi, was, " if not the most ancient, certainly the greatest, of the old Arlecchinos." He was the director of the *Accesi* and greatly in favour at the Court of Henry IV. of France. In October, 1611,

---

[1] Quoted Sand, *op. cit.*, Vol. I., p. 74.
[2] *Diverses Poésies.* Caen. 1612, p. 30.

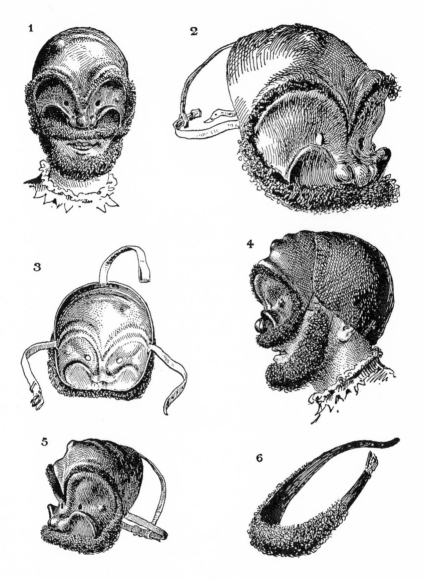

MASK OF AN ITALIAN HARLEQUIN (18TH CENTURY)

1. *Full-face.* 2. *Three-quarter.* 3. *Interior.* 4. *Profile.* 5. *Three-quarter.*
6. *Chin-piece.*

From drawings by Maurice Leloir of a mask in his collection

Marie de Medici stood godmother to his son. Martinelli was the author of that curious work, already mentioned, entitled *Compositions de Rhetorique*. In addition to his talents as an actor, he had a pleasant talent for writing letters,[1] which he seasoned with a wit not far removed from impertinence. He signed himself *Tristano Martinelli* or *Tristanus de Martinellis*. When he became a person of note he employed the signature *Arlechinus*, and at the height of his glory styled himself *Dominus Arlechinorum*. He died in 1630, at the age of seventy-seven.

Little is known of Giovanni Battista Andreini, the Harlequin of the *Fedeli*. He is said to have learned his art as a member of the *Gelosi*, which was managed by his father, Francesco Andreini. When his mother died and his father retired from the stage, he formed a new company called *I Comici Fedeli*. He came to Paris with his troupe in 1613 at the request of Marie de Medici. In the same year he composed a mystery entitled *Adamo*, which he dedicated to the Queen. When his father died, he wrote a pamphlet styled *Teatro Celeste*, in which he took solemn leave of the stage. This book consists of a number of sonnets ; one of them, in which he takes farewell of the stage, begins thus :

> False stage, I leave thee. Nevermore shall I stand in pride and splendour on thy boards. Yea, I leave all this empty show and at the same time withdraw from the beautiful land of France.[2] . . .

But his actions belied his words, for he continued to act until he had reached the age of seventy-three, when he retired with the title of Grand Huntsman to the Duke of Mantua.

The next Harlequin of note was Domenico Locatelli. He would appear to have come to Paris about 1644. He played the character of *Trivelino*, a part analogous to Harlequin. It will be noticed that his costume (see Pl. fcg. p. 50) differs little from that worn by Martinelli. He too was much liked at Court. He composed in

---

[1] See Baschet, *op. cit.*, pp. 204, 206, 219, 222, 234, 276, 277, 286, 288, and 301, for specimens of Martinelli's correspondence.
[2] Quoted Mantzius, *op. cit.*, Vol. II., p. 285.

French the scenario of a piece entitled *Rosaure, Imperatrice de Constantinople*, which was presented at the Theatre of the Petit Bourbon in 1658. Locatelli died on the 26th of April, 1671, at the age of fifty-eight.

Presently the part of Harlequin received a transformation by the interpretation of Domenico (Biancolelli). Giuseppe Domenico Biancolelli was born at Bologna in 1640. His parents were comedians in a troupe established in that city, and, when still a child, he assisted them in their performances. In 1659, Cardinal Mazarin, who, as we have noted, possessed a company of Italian actors and desired to add to their number, sent invitations to Italy for several comedians to join his troupe, including Biancolelli, who at that time was performing at Vienna in a company known as the *Tabarini*. In the Cardinal's troupe Harlequin was played in the traditional manner by Locatelli. Biancolelli arrived the following year and acted [1] as a kind of second Harlequin, continuing in that part until Locatelli's death.

Domenico, as he was called then, became a great personality, and was acclaimed the finest actor of his day. He was a person of wide reading and cultured wit, and transformed Harlequin from a mere coarse buffoon into an individual of wit and intelligence. He effected many changes in the traditional costume. He lengthened the jacket and widened the trousers. The parti-coloured patches were placed symmetrically; the hare's scut, the mask, bat, and belt remained as before. Sometimes the collar of the jacket was fringed with a miniature ruff. It is the costume rendered familiar by the paintings of Watteau and Lancret. Domenico had a peculiar defect in his speech which caused him to speak his lines with a kind of throaty croaking like that of a parrot.

There are innumerable anecdotes regarding Domenico. One evening at a royal supper, he regarded anxiously a certain dish of partridges. Louis XIV., observing his glance, said to a lackey :
" Let this dish be given to Domenico."
" And the partridges also ? " enquired Domenico.

[1] He made his first appearance in Paris in 1661.

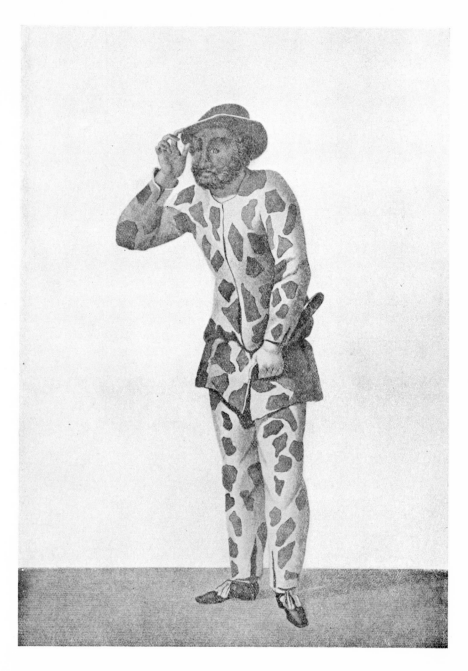

DOMENICO LOCATELLI AS TRIVELINO

" And the partridges also," replied the King, appreciating the comedian's ready wit.   The dish was of gold.

On another occasion, Louis XIV., returning from a hunting expedition, went incognito to attend the performance of an Italian piece that was being given at Versailles.

" That is a bad piece," he said to Domenico, as he was leaving.

" Whisper it," replied Domenico, " because if the King were to hear you he would dismiss me together with my troupe."

The celebrated Harlequin's anxiety to please the King brought upon him a fatal illness.   This was the result of a chill acquired by his executing a burlesque of a dance given by the King's *maître de ballet*, the famous Beauchamps.   The player's exertions caused him to sweat profusely, and having no opportunity to change his linen immediately, he caught a chill which developed into pneumonia.   He lay ill for eight days when, after having renounced the theatre, he died at six o'clock in the evening of the 2nd of August, 1688.   He was buried at Saint-Eustache, opposite the Chapel of the Virgin.

His comrades gave public expression to their great sorrow by closing their theatre for a whole month.   The reopening was prefaced with the following announcement :

We have long marked our sorrow by our silence, and we should prolong it further if the apprehension of displeasing you did not influence us more profoundly than our legitimate pain.   We shall reopen our theatre on Wednesday next, the 1st of September, 1688.   In the impossibility of repairing the loss we have sustained, we offer you of the best that our application and our care are able to supply.   Bear us a little indulgence and be assured that we shall omit nothing that will contribute to your pleasure.[1]

Domenico was succeeded in 1689 by Evaristo Gherardi.   He was the son of Giovanni Gherardi, an actor well known under the name of *Flautin*, and was born at Prato, in Tuscany, about 1666. At an early age he came to Paris where he received an excellent

---

[1] Quoted Sand, *op. cit.*, Vol. I., p. 78.

classical education at one of the best colleges. He made his first appearance on the 1st of October under the auspices of Tiberio Fiorilli, an intimate friend of his father's, as Harlequin in a play entitled *Le Divorce Forcé*. The young player was certainly bold in attempting this part, for Domenico himself had essayed the character in the preceding year, and, despite the wealth of his experience, had failed to score a success. Yet, by a strange twist of fortune, so frequently associated with theatrical ventures, Gherardi's performance was received with enthusiasm. Let us hear his own naïve comments upon the matter :—

This comedy *Le Divorce Forcé* had not succeeded in the hands of Domenico. It had been erased from the catalogue of plays which were revived from time to time, and the parts had been burnt. Nevertheless, despite that I had never been on the stage in my life, and that I had but just left the college of La Marche where I had just concluded my course of philosophy under the learned M. Bublé, I chose it for my first appearance which took place on the 1st of October, 1689. The piece was so successful in my hands that it gave pleasure to everyone, was extraordinarily well attended, and consequently earned a great deal of money for the company.

If I were the man to derive vanity from the theatrical talents which nature has given me, either with face uncovered or under a mask, in the leading serious or comic roles, I should have in this the most ample grounds upon which to flatter my self-esteem. I should say that I did more in my beginnings and in my first years than the most illustrious actors have been able to do after twenty years of experience, and in the full prime of their lives. But I protest that very far from having ever become elated by these rare advantages, I have always considered them to be the results of my good fortune, rather than the consequences of my merits ; and if anything has been able to flatter my soul in this connection, it is the pleasure of seeing myself universally applauded after the inimitable M. Domenico, who went so far in the expression of naïveté—that which the Italians call *goffagine*—of the character of Harlequin, that all those who witnessed his performance must always find some fault with the most famous Harlequin of any later day.[1]

[1] Quoted Campardon, *op. cit.*, Vol. I., pp. 240, 241.

Bologne est ma patrie et Paris mon Séjour,
J'y regne avec Éclat sur la Scène Comique,
Harlequin sous le masque y cache Dominique
Qui reforme en riant et le peuple et la Cour.

GIUSEPPE DOMENICO BIANCOLELLI (DOMENICO)
From the engraving by Hubert

The following description of his appearance is given in *Le Pompe Funèbre d'Arlechin* 1701 :

Je commence par son portrait.
Tu ne le vis que sous le masque,
et qu'avec son pourpoint de Basque ;
Il n'étoit ni bien, ni mal fait,
grand ni petit, plus gras que maigre :
il avait le corps alaigre.
Le front haut, l'œil foible, mais vif.
Le nez très-significatif,
et qui promettoit des merveilles.
La bouche atteignoit ses oreilles ;
son teint étoit d'homme de feu,
son menton se doubloit un peu,
son encolure assez petite
le menaçoit de mort subite.
Pour voir au vif son vrai portrait,
Il faut voir le fils qu'il a fait,
a mon avis il lui ressemble,
hormis qu'il est un peu vulcain,
ce que n'étoit pas arlequin,
ou pour le moins il me le semble.[1]

Gherardi achieved an excellent reputation and continued to attract huge audiences until the theatre was closed in 1697 for reasons which have been stated in a previous chapter. He exerted all his influence to get the theatre reopened, but without success. He thereupon devoted his time to writing out the *scenari* of the plays presented by his company. This work, entitled *Le Théâtre Italien de Gherardi*, was issued in six volumes and contains fifty-six plays " as given by the King's Italian comedians during the time they were in service."

Some months before his book was published, he accidentally fell on his head during a private performance at Saint-Maur. He treated the hurt as of no consequence, but on the 31st of August,

[1] Quoted Rasi (Luigi), *I Comici Italiani.* 2 Vols. 1894–1905. Vol. I., p. 1010.

1700, the very day he had been to present a copy of his work to Monseigneur, he had a seizure and died. He was buried the following day at Saints-Innocents Cemetery.

In 1716, a new troupe was summoned to Paris by command of the Regent. The Harlequin was Tomasso Antonio Vicentini,[1] known as Thomassin. He was born at Vicenza about 1683. At an early age he joined a company travelling through Italy and played tragic parts. It is also said of him that at Rome, where the appearance of women on the stage was forbidden, he acted the parts of young princesses to much applause. For some reason unknown to us, he forsook tragedy for comedy and became a Harlequin, in which character he soon acquired a considerable reputation. He made his first appearance in Paris on the 18th of May, 1716, in *L'Inganno Fortunato*, an Italian piece known in French as *L'Heureuse Surprise*.

There is an interesting anecdote regarding Thomassin's performance related by Gueullette, a contemporary playwright. As we know, Domenico had invested the character of Harlequin with an artificial manner of speaking. The public had become so accustomed to Harlequin's speaking thus, that they could not conceive of his speaking otherwise. Riccoboni and Thomassin, being advised of this tradition, were troubled greatly, especially the latter, who was accustomed to deliver his lines in a natural voice.

Now in *L'Heureuse Surprise* there are many scenes at night-time. One of them was placed at the beginning of the piece. Lelio calls for his valet Harlequin who at first does not reply, then answers at long intervals as if he went to sleep again between each response. Lelio, indignant, goes to fetch him, and brings him on the stage sleeping as he walks. At last Lelio succeeds in arousing him. But Harlequin has no sooner replied than he sinks to the ground and falls to sleep again. His master drags him up and Harlequin falls asleep on his arms. The spectators were so taken with this scene, that having laughed and applauded for a whole quarter of an

[1] Also written *Visentini*.

Evariste Gherardi.
dit Arlequin.

A Paris chez J. Mariette rue S.ᵗ Jacques aux

hour, they had not the heart to cavil when Harlequin spoke in his usual voice.

When the number of spectators at the Hôtel de Bourgogne began to thin, partly because they could not understand plays presented in Italian, and perhaps more so on account of the revival of certain old French pieces, the grossness of which had caused them to be omitted from the repertory of the old company, Thomassin still found favour with the public and helped to revive the waning interest.

He had a brilliant career. Agile, gay and always original, he would set the house in roars of laughter by some inimitable display of buffoonery, then, passing almost imperceptibly from comedy to tragedy, he would cause the same public to shed tears of sorrow— no light achievement when it is remembered that his face was covered by a mask. His physical dexterity was remarkable. In this respect he is said to have attained such a degree of perfection that he could turn a somersault with a full glass in his hand and alight on his feet without having spilt a single drop of the wine. Thomassin died on the 19th of August, 1739, and was buried in the church of Saint-Laurent.

There can be no doubt but that the Mask of Harlequin, which was more extemporaneous than any other, was a difficult part which required for its interpretation an exceptionally talented actor gifted with an agile and graceful body, and a mind stored with a fund of ready wit and invention. The spontaneous nature of the acting was in itself not without its drawbacks, for, as Ricco-boni asserts :

Improvisation is the stumbling block of Harlequins ; if they be witty, a word or a situation easily tempts them to wander away from the subject ; if not, they are compelled to resort to *doubles ententes* which are badly invented and worse delivered. They lack the fund of talent and knowledge which might teach them to use the poison without being infected by it. It is a very difficult art, and I do not advise any actor to choose this career.[1]

[1] Quoted Mantzius, *op. cit.*, Vol. II., p. 259.

Marmontel, writing in the eighteenth century, gives an interesting description of the Harlequin of his day :

His character presents a mixture of ignorance, naïveté, stupidity and grace. He is like a mere sketch of a man, a great child visited by flashes of reason and intelligence, in all of whose capers and awkwardnesses there is something sharp and interesting. The model Harlequin is all suppleness and agility, with the grace of a young cat, yet equipped with a superficial coarseness that renders his performances more amusing ; the part is that of a lackey, patient, faithful, credulous, gluttonous, always in love, always in difficulties either on his master's account or on his own, afflicting himself and consoling himself again with the readiness of a child, one whose sorrows are as amusing as his joys. Such a part demands a great deal of naturalness and of wit, and a great deal of physical grace and suppleness.[1]

On the 21st of November, 1739, Antonio Constantini, brother of Angelo Constantini, the celebrated Mezzetino, essayed the character of Harlequin, but not sufficiently well to be accepted as successor to Thomassin. This was only one of many unsuccessful attempts. A contemporary wrote :

It is altogether incredible what a number of Harlequins appeared within the space of three or four years, they seemed to rise from the ashes of Thomassin : but, similar to those shadows which are formed from the exhalations of tombs, and which the least sound dissipates, so all these disappeared before the booings of the groundlings.[2]

The next great Harlequin was Carlo Antonio Bertinazzi, called Carlin, who was born at Turin on the 2nd of December, 1710. He was the son of Felice Bertinazzi, an officer in the army of the King of Sardinia, and Giovanna Maria Gti. He was only three years old when his father died, but his mother gave him a thorough education which included fencing and dancing.

At fourteen he became an ensign, but conceiving a distaste for the military profession, and the death of his mother having freed him of family ties, he resigned his commission and became an actor.

[1] Quoted Sand, *op. cit.*, Vol. I., p. 75.
[2] *Id.*, Vol. I., p. 105.

Dans les Ris comme dans les pleurs,
Imitateur de la Nature,
Il sçait charmer les Spectateurs,
Et leur plait encore en peinture.

TOMASSO ANTONIO VICENTINI (THOMASSIN) AS ARLECCHINO

From the engraving after La Tour

Having studied his art for some time, he played the part of Harlequin with considerable success at theatres in Bologna and Venice. He was soon acclaimed one of the best players of the day, and the Italian comedians at Paris, being anxious to fill the gap created by the death of Thomassin, invited him to join them. Carlin arrived in Paris early in the year 1741, and on the 10th of April he made his bow before the Parisian public. Since he spoke little French, he selected Riccoboni's piece *Arlecchino muto per forza* for his first appearance. The day appointed was also that of the reopening of the theatre which according to custom had been closed during the Easter fortnight.

The new player was introduced to the audience by his comrade, Charles Raymond Richard de Bouillac, in the following terms :

Gentlemen, this day, which renews our efforts and our homage, was to have been marked by the novelty which we had prepared for you ; but the actor who is going to have the honour of appearing before you for the first time was too deeply interested, and too impatient to learn his fate, to permit us to postpone his *début*. " Should your novelty fail," said he, " I shall learn how your public hisses, and that is something that I do not want to learn ; should it succeed I shall know how they applaud, and I shall draw, perhaps, a sad comparison between its reception and that which may be accorded to me." In order not to give this new actor any grounds for reproach, we have conformed entirely with his wishes. He knows, gentlemen, not only what he has to dread in appearing before you, but also in following that excellent actor whom we have lost in whose *rôle* you are about to see him. These just causes of apprehension would be counterbalanced in his mind if he were aware of the resources which await him in your indulgence ; but it is in vain that we have endeavoured to reassure him on this score ; he can be convinced of the truth of it only by yourselves, and we hope, gentlemen, that you will be disposed to fulfil the promises which we have made to him on your behalf. They are founded upon an experience so long and so happy that we are as assured of your kindliness as you must be of our zeal and profound respect.[1]

Carlin made an excellent impression, and in the year following

[1] *Mercure de France.* April, 1741, p. 789.

he became a permanent member of the company, pleasing alike with the excellence of his miming and the charm of his dancing. He had an extraordinary prescience in divining the public taste, and the most solemn spectator was soon reduced to smiling at his sallies. He possessed the rare merit of appearing always different and always excellent. And like Thomassin, he could make the audience laugh one moment, and cry the next.

His *forte* was improvised comedy which afforded him abundant opportunity for the exercise of his brilliant wit and fertile imagination. David Garrick, who saw him perform at Paris, was charmed by his art, and, observing Carlin in a scene where Harlequin, having received a sound drubbing from his master, shakes his fist at the latter's retreating form, while with the other hand he rubs his bruised back, he exclaimed : " Behold how the very back of Carlin has a physiognomy and an expression." Bartoli describes his acting thus : " All he did was to change wigs, according to the character he performed, he wore a black wig or a grey (round) wig, or a third one, after the French fashion, with a pouch attached to it ; with this small, yet important change, and by disguising his voice and varying his carriage, many of the spectators never could understand that it was he alone who performed the three characters." [1]

Carlin was a well-informed man on many subjects ; he played several musical instruments, both painted well and engraved well, and wielded a skilful pen—witness his piece *Les Metamorphoses d'Arlequin*. An admirer wrote in 1751 the following verse in his honour :

> La vérité n'est point flatée :
> Oui Carlin paroît à nos yeux
> Ce que Momus est dans les cieux
> Ce que chez Neptune est Protée.[2]

Goldoni, speaking of Carlin in his Memoirs, declares that he

---

[1] Bartoli (F.), *Notizie istoriche de' comici italiani che fiorirono intorno all' anno MDL. fino a' giorni presenti.* 2 Vols. Padova. 1781. Quoted Mantzius. *Op. cit.*, Vol. II., p. 315.
[2] Quoted Campardon, *op. cit.*, Vol. I., p. 44.

De.Figh Delin.ᵗ

C.Grignion Sculp.ᵗ

Mʳ. CARLIN.

ARLEQUIN sortant de la mer dans le Prince de Salerne.
Comedie Italienne.

Published by Jefferys & Faden, the Corner of St Martins Lane Charing Cross.
as the Act directs 1 May 1773.

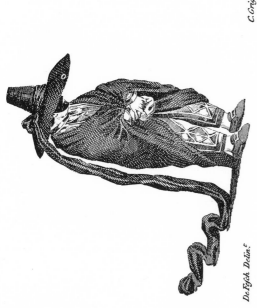

Mʳ. CARLIN.

ARLEQUIN en Deuil de son maitre dans le
Viellard amoureux.
Comedie Italienne

Published by Jefferys & Faden, Corner of St Martins Lane Charing Cross,
as the Act directs 1 May 1773.

CARLO BERTINAZZI (CARLIN) AS ARLECCHINO

From engravings in the collection of M. Willson Disher

" was in high estimation for his propriety of behaviour, celebrated as a Harlequin, and in the possession of a reputation which raised him to a level with Domenique and Thomassin in France, and Sacchi in Italy. Nature had endowed him with inimitable graces ; his figure, his gestures, his movements, prepossessed everyone in his favour. For his action and talents he was admired on the stage, and for his private character he was beloved in society." [1]

The pieces with which his name is inseparably associated are *Coraline Magicienne*, *Les Fées Rivales*, *Le Prince de Salerne* and *Les Vingt-six Infortunes d'Arlequin*, all by Veronese ; the two anonymous pieces, *Coraline Esprit Follet* and *La Joute d'Arlequin ;* and, in particular, *Le Fils d'Arlequin Perdu et Retrouvé*, by Goldoni.

Carlin died at Paris following an attack of apoplexy on the 6th of September, 1783. A few days later a journal published the following epitaph in his honour :

> De Carlin pour peindre le sort,
> Très-peu de mots doivent suffire :
> Tout sa vie il a fait rire,
> Il a fait pleurer à sa mort.[2]

No new Harlequin of any account appeared until 1757, when Bigottini, a native of Rome, made his bow at the Comédie Italienne on the 27th of April of that year in *Arlequin, maître de musique, ou le Capitaine Scanderburg*. He played also in *Arlequin Protée* and *Les Métamorphoses d'Arlequin*, but achieved such little success that he retired.

However, on the 25th of December, 1775, he received a command to rejoin the Comédie Italienne, but it was not until the 18th of February, 1777, that he played Harlequin in a play of his own composition entitled *Arlequin esprit follet*. This time he was more successful, and his efforts were greeted with applause. Grimm describes the performance thus :

The performance of the Sieur Bigottini has no analogy with that of the

---

[1] *Op. cit.*, Vol. II., pp. 143, 144.
[2] Quoted Campardon, *op. cit.*, Vol. I., p. 47.

actor he is replacing ; he has not the same grace nor the same subtlety, nor yet the same naïveté ; nevertheless his metamorphoses are ingenious and varied, and his movements, without having the suppleness which characterised the slightest gestures of Carlin, are of extraordinary precision and lightness. Nothing could equal the swiftness with which he changes his costume and mask, his talent in this is prodigious,[1] but it is a kind of merit which does not amuse us for very long, whatever surprise it may occasion at first sight. Miracles of this kind would suffice to make the fortune of a sorcerer or a prophet, but not that of a harlequin. The most ingeniously contrived tricks soon exhaust their powers of attraction. It is only wit that may be infinitely varied, it is only grace whose charm never stales.

But, as Grimm foresaw, the public soon tired of Bigottini as Harlequin, and he was instructed to play the Doctor instead, which he did moderately well. In 1780, he was pensioned off with the other Italian comedians.

After Bigottini, the Improvised Comedy declined gradually, and disappeared. For a time, some of the original Masks retained their character and costume, others, as a result of their French environment, acquired new qualities and were baptized again : for example, Pierrot became *Gilles*, Pantalone was called *Cassandre*, and so on. The later plays given in Paris by the Italians consisted, as formerly, of a scanty outline of the plot which provided the basis for improvisations. But, in addition, specially written scenes would be interpolated. These were memorised by the actors and recited.

By the beginning of the eighteenth century good mimes had become rare, singing began to encroach on the dialogue, and, as a consequence, the performance developed more and more into a species of comic opera. Harlequin's miming began to lose its zest ; his antics to cast off their racy, native humour. He weakened year by year to become in the nineteenth century the emasculated, artificial creature, recognisable by his costume alone, that we see in the drawings and lithographs of Chéret, Morin and Willette.

[1] Goldoni (*op. cit.*, I., 305) says Bigottini was " a good actor in the parts suited to his character ; but he was surprising for the changes and transformations he went through."

COSTUME, MASK AND BAT OF AN ITALIAN HARLEQUIN
(18TH CENTURY)

In the collection of Maurice Leloir

In Italy, the principal Harlequins were Fremeri (1624), Belotti (1625), Francesco (1630), Astori (1720), Bertoli (1730), Ignazio Casanova (1734), Giacinto Cattoli (1739), Antonio Sacchi (1788), and lastly Golinetti, who appeared at the close of the same century.

Giacinto Cattoli, a native of Bologna, was an actor in the service of Antonio Farnese, Grand Duke of Parma, and held in great esteem for his acting of a variation of the Harlequin Mask known as *Tracagnino*. He began his career in the Duke of Mantua's company in which he remained until 1708, when he went to Venice. He was at Bologna in 1716 and again in 1739, when he died in December. On the 27th of that month he was buried with great pomp in the Church of St. Michele del Mercato, his bier escorted by all the *Tracagnini*, who universally mourned him, carrying lighted torches.

But of all these Harlequins, Sacchi [1] was indubitably the greatest artist. He was a Ferrarese, born at Vienna in 1708. He was noted also as the *Capocomico* of a famous troupe of comedians which included Agostino Fiorilli (*Tartaglia*), Atanasio Zannoni (*Brighella*), and Cesare D'Arbes (*Pantalone*). Sacchi's great period was from 1740 to 1770. He invented the Mask of *Truffaldino*,[2] a specific type of Harlequin.

Carlo Gozzi, who was associated with him for some twenty-five years in the dual capacity of playwright and adviser, gives in his Memoirs many interesting details of Sacchi's career and pays many tributes to the actor's perfection in his art. " No one," says Gozzi, " may write the part of *Truffaldino*, either in prose or verse. It suffices Sacchi to know the intention of the author, so as to enable him to improvise scenes superior to any which a writer might have prepared him."

Goldoni, though opposed to the *Commedia dell' Arte*, was no less appreciative, and remarks of him :

Sacchi possessed a lively and brilliant imagination ; he played in comedies of intrigue ; but while other harlequins merely repeated themselves,

---

[1] Also written *Sacco, Skagy.*
[2] *Truffa*—the crafty.

Sacchi, who always adhered to the essence of the play, contrived to give an air of freshness to the piece, by his new sallies and unexpected repartees. It was Sacchi alone whom the people crowded to see.

His comic traits, and his jests, were neither taken from the language of the lower orders nor that of the comedians. He levied contributions on comic authors, on poets, orators, and philosophers ; and in his impromptus we could recognize the thoughts of Seneca, Cicero or Montaigne ; but he possessed the art of appropriating the maxims of these great men to himself, and allying them to the simplicity of the blockhead ; and the same proposition which was admired in a serious author became highly ridiculous in the mouth of this excellent actor.[1]

[1] *Op. cit.*, Vol. I., p. 281.

GIACINTO CATTOLI AS ARLECCHINO

From the design by Giuliano Rost

Chapter Seven

Harlequin Scenes from the Repertory of the Italian Comedians

SCENE: HARLEQUIN & PASQUARIELLO

HARLEQUIN (*dressed half like a woman and half like a man, appears at the back of a Draper's shop which adjoins that of a Lemonade-Seller.*)

HARLEQUIN (*showing the half of him that is in woman's dress, and imitating a Draper, cries :*) Shirts, neckerchiefs, drawers and dusters, Gentlemen.

PASQUARIELLO. Ah here is a draper's shop. I am in need of some linen. I will see if she has what I require.

HARLEQUIN. This way, Sir, beautiful Holland cloth, fine bedroom slippers proof against sweat.

PASQUARIELLO (*taking a shirt which he finds on the counter, and looking at* HARLEQUIN, *says :*) I should be pleased to buy something from you. (*Aside.*) This girl is pretty, well made. What beautiful blue eyes !

HARLEQUIN (*who has only heard the last words*). Blue, Sir ? I assure you that there are no blue marks in my linen.

PASQUARIELLO (*examining the shirt*). This shirt would suit me fairly well, but I fear it is too small.

HARLEQUIN. Small, Sir ? Surely not, it is three and a half quarters [1] long.

---

[1] The quarter of a yard : nine inches.

PASQUARIELLO (*looking at* HARLEQUIN—*aside*). What a beautiful nose ! [1]

HARLEQUIN. It is well measured, don't you worry, my ell is nearly an inch longer than that of others.

PASQUARIELLO. What do you ask for it ?

HARLEQUIN. It will cost you ten crowns, and that is not too much.

PASQUARIELLO. Ten crowns !

HARLEQUIN. Yes, Sir. Honestly, I do not make more than a livre on the sol.

PASQUARIELLO. I will give you thirty sols.

HARLEQUIN. Thirty sols ! It is easy to see that you are not used to wearing shirts.

PASQUARIELLO. Here is a crown and no more bargaining ! Do not let me go elsewhere if you can help it.

HARLEQUIN. All right, take it, but on condition that you will do me the honour of coming back to my shop. It is at the Sign of the Virgin. It is I, Sir, who supplies the baby-linen for the children of the eunuchs of the Grand Harem.

PASQUARIELLO. What is your name ?

HARLEQUIN. I am called the beautiful Angélique, at your service.

PASQUARIELLO. I am obliged to you. I hope to see you again.

HARLEQUIN (*turns the half of him that is in man's dress and appears in the shop of the Lemonade-Seller, when he cries :*) Biscuits, lemonade, macaroons, coffee, iced chocolate, Gentlemen. (*To* PASQUARIELLO :) Psst, psst, Sir. (PASQUARIELLO *turns towards him.*) One word, if you please. (PASQUARIELLO *approaches.*) Apparently, Sir, you are a stranger. Don't worry yourself with that old cow next door. She will trick you. Her shop is only frequented by worthless fellows of every class. (PASQUARIELLO

---

[1] This sentence contains a pun which cannot be rendered into English, the words *beau nez* (beautiful nose) and *bien aulné* (well measured) have a somewhat similar sound.

ANTONIO SACCHI AS ARLECCHINO

From an old engraving

raises his shoulders in astonishment. At this moment HARLEQUIN *re-enters the Draper's shop and shows the half of him that is in woman's dress, takes* PASQUARIELLO *by the arm, and says :*) What has that poisoner of the human race told you ? There's a fine rascal to call me a cow ! What is a Lemonade-Seller's shop, my friend ? It consists of two buckets of water, a couple of lemons and an ounce of sugar.

(PASQUARIELLO *tries to speak, when* HARLEQUIN *goes into the other shop and appears as the Lemonade-Seller.*)

HARLEQUIN (*talking at the Draper*). It is true that a Draper's shop is much better stocked. Of thirty packets in her shop, there are not four filled with goods. Witness the donkey that being tied to her door the other day, ate six that were only filled with hay.

PASQUARIELLO (*to the Lemonade-Seller*). But, Sir . . .

HARLEQUIN (*as the Draper, always talking at the Lemonade-Seller*). As you supply drink, I am happy to supply food. For he who drinks water can very well eat hay.

PASQUARIELLO (*to the Draper*). But, Madam . . .

HARLEQUIN (*in the Lemonade-Seller's, always talking at the Draper*). Quiet there, seller of English point lace made in Paris !

PASQUARIELLO. Again . . .

HARLEQUIN (*as the Draper*). Quiet there, seller of Roman lemonade ! If that were so, Rome was built on the Seine.

PASQUARIELLO. If you please . . .

HARLEQUIN (*as the Lemonade-Seller*). That wouldn't be in your shop, for you are not healthy.[1] We all know about you.

PASQUARIELLO. Do not listen. . . .

HARLEQUIN (*as the Draper*). Go away ! Seller of Levant coffee. Go and sell it in the West for you're as drunk as an owl.

PASQUARIELLO. You must not . . .

HARLEQUIN (*as the Lemonade-Seller*). You have a long tongue ; if your ell measure were the same, buyers would not complain as they do.

[1] This sentence contains a pun which cannot be rendered into English, the words *Seine* and *saine* (healthy) have a similar sound.

PASQUARIELLO. Again, must I . . .

HARLEQUIN (*as the Draper*). I'll show you whether my ell is the right measure. (*He takes the stick and, pretending to aim a blow at the Lemonade-Seller, hits* PASQUARIELLO.)

PASQUARIELLO. Indeed, this is too much !

HARLEQUIN (*as the Lemonade-Seller*). Yes, I'll teach you to raise your hand on a man like me. (*He takes an earthenware pot and, pretending to throw it at the Draper, hits* PASQUARIELLO *on the head. After two or three repetitions of this* lazzi, HARLEQUIN *comes out as the Lemonade-Seller as if he wished to throw himself on the Draper, he turns so quickly from one side to the other that* PAS-QUARIELLO, *seeing a man on one side and a woman on the other, truly believes them to be fighting and hastens to separate them, and so receives many blows. After this,* HARLEQUIN *exits laughingly and leaves* PASQUARIELLO *on the ground who, on rising, says :* These people are very irritated with one another, *and goes off.*)

(From *Arlequin Lingère du Palais*, Scene I.[1] A Comedy in Three Acts. Produced by M. D * * * , and first performed by the King's Italian Comedians at the Hôtel de Bourgogne, the 4th of October, 1682.)

SCENE : THE DESPAIR OF HARLEQUIN

HARLEQUIN. Ah ! How unfortunate I am ! The Doctor wishes to marry Columbine to a Farmer, and how can I live without Columbine ? No, I would sooner die. What an ignorant Doctor ! What an inconstant Columbine ! What a knavish Farmer ! What an extremely miserable Harlequin ! Let me

---

[1] Gherardi, *op. cit.*, Vol. I., p. 55.

EVARISTO GHERARDI

From Gherardi's " Histoire du Théâtre Italien," 1741

hasten to die. It shall be written in ancient and modern history :
Harlequin died for Columbine. I shall go to my room, attach a
rope to a beam, climb on to a chair, tie the rope round my neck,
give a kick to the chair, and behold me hanged ! (*He assumes the
attitude of a person hanged.*)   It is done, nothing can stop me, let
us hasten to the gallows. . . . To the gallows ? Fie on you, Sir,
you must not think of it. To kill yourself for a girl, that would
be a fine piece of foolishness. . . . Yes, Sir ; but for a girl to
deceive an honest man, that is a rascally trick. . . . Agreed, but
when you are hanged, will you be any fatter ? . . . No, I shall be
thinner ; I desire a slender figure. What have you to say to that ?
If you want to join me, you have but to come. . . . Oh, as for
that, no ; but you are not going. . . . Oh, but I am. . . . Oh no,
you are not. . . . But I am going, I tell you. (*He draws his sword
with which he strikes himself, then cries :*) There ! I am rid of that
troublesome fellow. Now that there is no one to interfere with
me I shall go and hang myself. (*He makes as if to go, then stops
short.*)   But no ! To hang, is an ordinary death, such as one sees
every day, I should gain little glory in it. Let us seek some
extraordinary kind of death, a death befitting a Harlequin. (*He
ponders.*) Ah ! I have it ! I shall stop up my nose and mouth, so
that the air cannot enter, and like that I shall die. There ! It is
done. (*He stops up his nose and mouth with his hands, and, after
having remained in this pose for some time, he says :*) No, the air
still escapes, it is not worth the trouble. Alas ! how hard it is to
die. (*He addresses the Pit.*) Sirs, if any amongst you would be
so kind as to die, so as to afford me a model, I should be infinitely
obliged. . . . I'faith, I have it. We read in history that there
have been people who have died of laughter. If I could die from
laughing, that would be a very droll death. I am very ticklish ;
if some one were to tickle me for long, they would make me die of
laughter. I shall go and tickle myself and thus I shall die. (*He
tickles himself, laughs and falls down.* PASQUARIELLO *comes, and
finding him so, believes him drunk, calls him, makes him rise, consoles
him and leads him away.*)

69

NOTE.—*Wherever in this scene, a sentence is followed by dots, it is understood that* HARLEQUIN *is to change his voice and gesture, sometimes going to one side and sometimes to the other.* *Those who witnessed this scene agree that it is one of the most diverting ever played at the* Théâtre Italien.

(From *Arlequin Empereur dans la Lune*, Scene II.[1] A Comedy in Three Acts. Produced by M. D * * * and first performed by the King's Italian Comedians at the Hôtel de Bourgogne, the 5th of March, 1684.)

SCENE : SOTINET, HARLEQUIN (*dressed as a Barber*) & MEZZETINO

HARLEQUIN (*to* SOTINET). They told me, Sir, that you had need of a member of my profession ; I come to offer you my services.

SOTINET. Ah, Sir, I am delighted to see you. Shave me, if you please, as quickly as you can.

HARLEQUIN. Don't worry, Sir, in two hours it will be done.

SOTINET. What do you mean by two hours ? I believe you're laughing at me.

HARLEQUIN. Oh, don't be astonished. I have been three whole months shaving a beard, and whilst I shaved one side, the hair grew again on the other, but now I'm more skilful, you'll see. (*He lays out his implements, takes off his cloak and puts it round* SOTINET'S *neck in place of a towel.*)

SOTINET. But what's this you've put round my neck ?

HARLEQUIN. I'faith, I beg your pardon. My haste to shave you made me take my cloak instead of a towel. Come along there, give me a towel, quick ! (MEZZETINO *gives him a towel.*)

[1] Gherardi, *op. cit.*, Vol. I., p. 114.

HARLEQUIN WEEPING

From the engraving after Claude Gillot

SOTINET (*looking at* MEZZETINO). Who is that man ?

HARLEQUIN. That's Master Jacques who looks after my implements. Come, Master Jacques, sharpen this razor for me, so that I can shave the gentleman. (MEZZETINO *takes the razor, and imitating a knife-grinder, moves his leg like the wheel of the grindstone and mimics with his mouth the noise that the razor makes when it is placed on the stone to sharpen it, and that made by the drops of water which fall on the wheel during the sharpening.* HARLEQUIN *explains all this to* SOTINET. *After several* lazzi *of this kind,* MEZZETINO *sings an Italian air, then, giving the razor to* HARLEQUIN, *says to him :* The purse is on this side, don't miss it, *and then goes.*)

SOTINET. What a pleasant man !

HARLEQUIN. Now then, Sir, I've not much time to lose. Sit down there. (*He pushes him roughly into a chair and taking him by the nose, puts barnacles on him.*)

SOTINET (*crying out*). Ooh ! Ooh ! Ooh ! (*He snatches off the barnacles and throws them on the ground.*) What the devil are you doing ? Do you take me for a horse ?

HARLEQUIN. Not at all, Sir, but some people are terribly restive under the steel, and this instrument would cut their throats if they said a word.

SOTINET. Indeed, I quite believe it.

HARLEQUIN (*takes a basin fashioned in a certain form and places it under* SOTINET'S *chin in order to shave him*).

SOTINET (*taking the basin*). What's this ?

HARLEQUIN. It's a double-handled basin. (HARLEQUIN *washes him and from time to time slaps him, then he draws forth a large ball which he uses to soap him with, and after having well rubbed* SOTINET'S *face he falls over one of his feet.*)

SOTINET. What are you doing that for ? Do you want to cripple me ? (*He gets up.*)

HARLEQUIN (*violently pushing* SOTINET *back in the chair*). What a babbler ! Sit still then ! Do you think I've only you to shave ? (*He shaves him with a razor of fearsome size.*)

SOTINET. Softly ! You're flaying me alive.

HARLEQUIN. That's because your hide is so tough that you notch all my razors. (*He takes a strop, hooks one end to* SOTINET'S *collar, holding the other in his left hand ; and, in order to gain more purchase to strop the razor he holds in his right hand, he raises one foot and plants it roughly in* SOTINET'S *stomach, and then, pulling the end of the leather with all his might, strops his razor so that he strangles* SOTINET, *who can scarcely call out.*)

SOTINET. Mercy ! You're killing me ! Help ! I'm being strangled ! (*He rises to call for help.*)

HARLEQUIN (*taking hold of him and obliging him to sit anew in the chair*). Plague take you ! If you move, I'll cut your throat. What sort of a man are you ?

SOTINET (*in a low voice*). I must submit, this scoundrel will do as he says ; he has an evil countenance. (*Aloud, while* HARLEQUIN *shaves him.*) Tell me, my friend, where do you come from ?

HARLEQUIN. From Limoges, Sir, at your service.

SOTINET. From Limoges ! Are there barbers in that country ? I thought there were only Gascons.

HARLEQUIN. I believe I'm the first of my countrymen to adopt the calling of barber. Formerly I was a stone-cutter, and as it was said that my hand was too light, I thought it better to adopt this profession. (*He puts his hand in* SOTINET'S *pocket.*) And once a stone-cutter, I am now a beard-cutter.

SOTINET (*surprising* HARLEQUIN'S *hand in his pocket*). It seems to me that your left hand is lighter than your right.

HARLEQUIN. Ah, Sir, you're laughing at me. These are little gifts one receives from nature, and of which an honest man doesn't boast.

(From *Le Divorce*, Act I., Scene IV.[1] A Comedy in Three Acts. Produced by M. Regnard and first performed by the King's Italian Comedians at the Hôtel de Bourgogne, the 17th of March, 1688.)

[1] Gherardi, *op. cit.*, Vol. II., p. 97.

HARLEQUIN SCENES FROM THE "COMMEDIA DELL' ARTE"

From Gherardi's " Histoire du Théâtre Italien," 1717

SCENE : THE OLD MAN, HIS WIFE & HARLEQUIN

THE OLD MAN. Ah ! Sir, isn't it a pity to be as beautiful as she is at twenty and yet be unable to have children ?

HARLEQUIN. And what is your temperament, my pretty one ? Melancholic, bilious ?

THE WIFE (*laughing*). Melancholic, I melancholic ? Ah, ah !

HARLEQUIN. What is your temperament then ?

THE WIFE. I haven't one. I dance, I sing, I drink a little, I take snuff, and if I had a husband who gave me as much money and pleasure as I wished, I should never worry at anything.

HARLEQUIN (*to the* OLD MAN). You are her father, apparently ?

THE OLD MAN. No, Sir. I haven't the honour to be the father of any one. I am her husband.

HARLEQUIN. Her husband ! Goodness, how old are you ?

THE OLD MAN. Seventy-seven on the 19th of April.

HARLEQUIN. Seventy-seven ! (*To the* WIFE.) And how do you get on with him ?

THE WIFE. I ? The best way in the world. My little husband has an income of twenty thousand livres, he has already given me half of it, and the usufruct of all if I have a child. Oh, I shall omit nothing to prevent our wealth from going to strangers.

THE OLD MAN. What a misfortune if I leave my estate to cousins eight times removed.

HARLEQUIN. Perhaps these cousins are nearer to you than your wife's children.

THE OLD MAN. Our cousins may laugh, but in nine months' time I shall show them an heir.

HARLEQUIN. That is being very positive.

THE OLD MAN. Oh, I have a prescription now.

THE WIFE. We have been told of a remedy. If we had only known at first !

HARLEQUIN. You have been seventy-seven years without finding the remedy ! I'faith, the malady is incurable. But may one inquire what the remedy is ?

THE WIFE. Good! There is hardly a woman that hasn't used it.

HARLEQUIN. For that cure, certain women employ remedies which are hardly approved by husbands.

THE WIFE. Oh, this one is an innocent remedy.

THE OLD MAN. Most innocent, Chalybeate water. . . .

HARLEQUIN. I know all about it.

THE OLD MAN. Can you believe that a neighbouring nobleman had not had any children during twenty-four years of married life ?

HARLEQUIN. Indeed !

THE WIFE. Chalybeate water gave him one.

HARLEQUIN. Let us understand one another. Did his wife drink Chalybeate water ?

THE OLD MAN. Yes.

HARLEQUIN. At home ?

THE WIFE. Not at all, it is only effective at the spring.

HARLEQUIN. Was her husband with her ?

THE OLD MAN. No, he sent his valet to keep her company.

HARLEQUIN. Very good. A most innocent remedy. Go, my good man. Take my advice and go home, and leave alone such waters which are only suitable for improving the busts of actresses and for curing dropsy in certain young ladies of evil reputation.

THE WIFE. But, Sir . . .

HARLEQUIN. Farewell. Be off with you.

(From *Arlequin Misantrope*, Act II., Scene VI.[1] A Comedy in Three Acts. Produced by M. de B * * * and first performed by the King's Italian Comedians at the Hôtel de Bourgogne, the 22nd of December, 1696.)

[1] Gherardi, *op. cit.*, Vol. VI., p. 427.

HARLEQUIN A GLUTTON
From the engraving after Claude Gillot

SCENE : ISABELLE, HARLEQUIN & COLUMBINE

HARLEQUIN (*looking at* COLUMBINE). She looks very nice.

COLUMBINE. If anything can console me for my ill luck, it is the hope of entering the service of a lady as good and as reasonable as yourself.

HARLEQUIN (*aside*). She is by no means a fool.

COLUMBINE. The Countess of Megret will tell you, Madam, that I have fought for a long time against the shame of going into service and that my distaste for it has been overcome by the honour of serving you.

ISABELLE. What a witty speech !

HARLEQUIN. Her face is no less witty.

ISABELLE. My child, young and delicate as you are, I am sure that there will not be too much work for you. You must arrange my hair, dress me, tie my ribbons, and, in addition, we have a quantity of linen to launder.

HARLEQUIN (*in a low voice to* COLUMBINE). Come to my house. I have only three shirts.

COLUMBINE (*to* ISABELLE). My age and temperament, Madam, will never permit me to do all you require.

ISABELLE. This girl charms me. What do you say. Colonel ?

HARLEQUIN. Well, she seems to be willing enough. *n a low voice to* ISABELLE.) Do you wish me to speak plainly ? She's not the girl for you, she's only a child. She would make a nice lover for my valet or my butler. But once these wretches fall in love, God knows how it will end.

COLUMBINE (*aside*). Cowardly knave !

HARLEQUIN (*to* ISABELLE). Take a good, buxom wench, strong and ugly. You'll be a thousand times better served. (*Turning towards* COLUMBINE.) I am speaking in your favour.

COLUMBINE. People of quality are always obliging. (*Aside.*) The scoundrel !

ISABELLE. It's no good your talking, this girl is quite to my liking, and I am going to beg my father to agree to my taking her.

(*She goes and when she reaches the " wings," returns to the Marquis, whom she has left alone with* COLUMBINE, *and says :*) Marquis, during my absence, at least, don't be frolicsome or forget yourself.

HARLEQUIN. How could you, my Princess! Can my heart feel joyful from the moment it loses sight of you? (*To* COLUMBINE, ISABELLE *having gone out.*) Listen, my girl, do you believe me? Don't poke yourself in this plaguey house, you would kill yourself in three days.

COLUMBINE. Ah, Sir, I have no choice in my present extremity. Since I am sent here, I must remain here.

HARLEQUIN. You're mad! Come and live with me, I shall adore you.

COLUMBINE. Haven't I got enough admirers? It would be very risky for a girl to lend ear to a man about to marry.

HARLEQUIN. That's the right time, my love. As soon as I have got my marriage portion, I will furnish a room for you from one end to the other. I will give you a little page and I will clothe you, you will see. Don't refuse to make your fortune. Of all the Marquises in France, I am, without any conceit, the most liberal.

COLUMBINE. I should be mad to believe you after the story of what happened to a certain COLUMBINE, men might rain down on me and I wouldn't pick up one.

HARLEQUIN. What!

COLUMBINE. I have been told that this poor creature fell in love with one called Har . . . Har . . . HARLEQUIN.

HARLEQUIN. Who is this beast HARLEQUIN?

COLUMBINE. It is said that he is a scamp, a parasite, a miserable wretch who ought to kiss the ground she has walked on.

HARLEQUIN. You're laughing at me.

COLUMBINE. No, no, Sir. It is not a joke. This rascal, despite all his vows and promises, left COLUMBINE and a few days ago put on all the airs of a Marquis.

HARLEQUIN (*aside*). Ouf!

COLUMBINE. They say he is on the eve of marrying the

WATTEAU'S ARLEQUIN

*From " L'Œuvre d'Antoine Watteau gravé par les soins de M. de Julienne," folio
(undated), in the British Museum*

daughter of a middle-class man who has given her a dowry of more than thirty thousand crowns.

HARLEQUIN. Is it possible ?

COLUMBINE. It is so very possible, that poor COLUMBINE has died of grief. After that, how can one trust a man's word ?

HARLEQUIN. In truth, there are a great many scoundrels in the world. But is she really dead ?

COLUMBINE. It is only too true.

HARLEQUIN (*aside*). So much the better. (*To* COLUMBINE.) Listen ! In that story there is something for and something against, yes. All I can tell you is that a man is a fool when he prefers his welfare to his pleasure. Since he loved COLUMBINE no more, has he not done well to provide for himself elsewhere ? In love, as in other things, wishes are free.

COLUMBINE (*making herself known*). *Perfidio, traditore, m'avrai negli occhi se non m'hai nel core*[1] (*and goes*).

HARLEQUIN. *Hoime ! Aiuto ! Spiriti ! Demoni !*

(From *Colombine Avocat Pour et Contre*, Act I., Scene X.[2] A Comedy in Three Acts. Produced by M. D * * * and first performed by the King's Italian Comedians at the Hôtel de Bourgogne, the 8th of June, 1685.)

SCENE : HARLEQUIN & PASQUARIELLO

PASQUARIELLO (*seeing* HARLEQUIN *perplexed to find a good means of livelihood*). Be a doctor, if fortune smiles on you, you'll soon be rich. It is one of the most lucrative of professions. Consider how much the Doctor has earned since gout has become the

[1] Perfidious traitor, you shall have me in your sight if not in your heart.
[2] Gherardi, *op. cit.*, Vol. I., p. 279.

fashion. He has amassed more than two hundred thousand francs, and he knows no more about it than you do.

HARLEQUIN. He must know precious little then, for I know nothing.

PASQUARIELLO. That should not hinder you from becoming a clever doctor.

HARLEQUIN. I'faith, you mock me! I can neither read nor write.

PASQUARIELLO. No matter, I say. It is not knowledge which makes the lucky doctor. It is impudence and high-flown language.

HARLEQUIN. If that be so, I shall soon ride in my carriage. I am as impudent as a devil; and as for language I often do not understand what I say myself. But must one know the methods doctors use and how they deal with their patients?

PASQUARIELLO. I am going to show you all that in a moment. You begin by having a mule and promenading all Paris on it. First comes a man who says: Sir doctor, I pray you to come and see a relation of mine who is ill. . . . Willingly, Sir. The man goes on in front and the doctor follows on his mule. (*Here* PASQUARIELLO *imitates the man who walks, and says to* HARLEQUIN *who follows him :*) What are you doing?

HARLEQUIN. I am the mule.

PASQUARIELLO. You arrive at the patient's house. The man knocks, the door is opened; the doctor dismounts from his mule and together they ascend the staircase.

HARLEQUIN. And the mule? Does the mule go up the staircase too?

PASQUARIELLO. No, no, the mule remains at the door. It is the man and the doctor who go up the stairs. Now they are in the room leading to that in which is the patient. The man says to the doctor: Follow me, Sir, I will go and see if my relative is asleep. (*Here* PASQUARIELLO *walks on tip-toe, stretches out one arm and pretends to draw aside the bed-curtains.*)

HARLEQUIN. Why do you step so softly?

HARLEQUIN SIGHING

From the engraving after Claude Gillot

PASQUARIELLO. On account of the sick man. We are now in his room and beside the bed.

HARLEQUIN. Beside his bed ? Be careful not to overturn anything.

PASQUARIELLO. Sir, the sick man is not asleep, you may approach. Immediately the doctor takes the armchair by the bedside and says to the patient : Show me your tongue. (PASQUARIELLO *puts out his tongue, and, imitating the patient, says :*) Oh Sir, I am very ill.

HARLEQUIN (*seeing this*). What a nasty illness !

PASQUARIELLO. The tongue is very dry and feverish.

HARLEQUIN. It must be put on ice.

PASQUARIELLO. How is the pulse ? (*He pretends to feel the patient's pulse.*) Now here is a pulse which goes devilish quickly.

HARLEQUIN. That surprises me, for usually pulses [1] move very slowly.

PASQUARIELLO. Let us feel the stomach. (*He pretends to feel the stomach.*) This is a very hard stomach.

HARLEQUIN. Perhaps he has swallowed some iron.

*   *   *   *   *

PASQUARIELLO. Let me have paper, pen and ink. (*He pretends to write.*) I will write a prescription : This evening give him an enema, to-morrow morning let him be bled, and to-morrow evening give him a dose of medicine. (*All this is mimed by* PASQUARIELLO *as if he were administering an enema, a blood-letting and swallowing medicine.*) Then you take leave of the patient and depart saying : Sir, to-morrow I shall visit you at the same hour, and I hope in a short time to restore you completely to health. Immediately the man who introduced you sees you to the door and slips a golden half-louis into your hand. You remount your mule and proceed.

HARLEQUIN. I find that very easy, but there is one thing that troubles me.

---

[1] This sentence contains a pun which cannot be rendered into English. The words *pouls* (pulse) and *poux* (lice) have a similar sound.

PASQUARIELLO. What is that ?

HARLEQUIN. It is how to feel a pulse. I am not used to that, and I should never be able to find out whether he has fever.

PASQUARIELLO. I will show you. When the pulse is regular, that is to say, when it goes tac, tac, tac, there is no fever. But when it is intermittent, or goes quickly, ti, ta, ta ; ti, ta, ta ; ti, ta, ta, there is fever.

HARLEQUIN. That's easy, tac, tac, tac, no fever ; ti, ta, ta ; ti, ta, ta ; ti, ta, ta, fever. Fever is like a horse when it gallops ; ti, ta, ta.

PASQUARIELLO. You are as wise as the doctors, let us go.

HARLEQUIN (*as he goes*). Ti, ta, ta ; ti, ta, ta. I am all for the ti, ta, ta.

(From *Arlequin Chevalier du Soleil*, Scene I.[1] A Comedy in Three Acts. Produced by M. D * * * and first performed by the King's Italian Comedians at the Hôtel de Bourgogne, the 26th of February, 1685.)

[1] Gherardi, *op. cit.*, Vol. I., p. 195.

TOMBEAU DE MAITRE ANDRÉ

Arlequin, quelque tems nous paru s'attendrir; Par des pleurs superflus cessant de s'affoiblir;
Mais jugeant la douleur inutile et maligne, Il se borne avorter les larmes de la vigne.

HARLEQUIN SCENE FROM THE "COMMEDIA DELL' ARTE"

From the engraving after Claude Gillot

Chapter Eight

Reasons for the Decline of the " Commedia dell' Arte "

IT is of interest to examine briefly the reasons for the decline of the improvised comedy on its native soil. It is clear that when the actor himself built upon a skeleton plot the entire character of the *rôle* assumed, the quality and strength of the impersonation rested on his own efforts.

At the best period of the *Commedia dell' Arte*, the seventeenth and first half of the eighteenth centuries, the player, when he was an artist and an idealist, fashioned a work probably unequalled for its novelty and forceful realism ; a conception spiced with keen wit, emphasised by wonderful miming and relieved by burlesqued movements which set the audience in a continual roar of laughter.

Companies of reputed actors could be certain of a packed theatre wherever they played. Exaggerated reports of their receipts spread to the smallest villages, and the love of gain caused the formation of innumerable troupes composed of spurious talent recruited from the worst characters of society. Devoid of merit, these motley bands took advantage of the privileged freedom earned by the true art to make their performance an open parade of the vilest obscenities. The Church, which had regarded with an unfriendly eye the *Commedia dell' Arte* from its inception, now classed it on a level with prostitutes, thieves and brigands. Even the great Domenico, lying on his death-bed in Paris, sought salvation by renouncing the theatre.

In Italy, the vagrant actors of the market-places were the foulest gang imaginable, if we credit the description cited by Symonds [1] from Garzoni's *Piazza Universale* :

No sooner have they made their entrance than the drum beats to let all the world know that the players are arrived. The first lady of the troupe, decked out like a man, with a sword in her right hand, goes round, inviting the folk to a comedy or tragedy or pastoral in the precincts of the Pellegrino. The populace, inquisitive by nature and eager for any new thing, hurries to take places. Paying their pennies down, they crowd into a hall, where a temporary stage has been erected, the scenes scrawled with charcoal as chance and want of sense will have it. An orchestra of tongs and bones, like the braying of asses or the caterwauling of cats in February, performs the overture. Then comes a prologue in the manner of a quack-doctor's oration to his gulls. The piece opens ; you behold a Magnifico, who is not worth the quarter of a farthing ; a Zanni, who straddles like a goose ; a Gratiano, who squirts his words out from a clyster-pipe ; a lover, who acts like a narcotic on the senses of his neighbours ; a Spanish captain, with nothing but a couple of musty oaths in his whole repertory ; a stupid and foul-mouthed bawd ; a pedant, who trips up in Tuscan phrases at each turn ; a Burattino, whose whole humour consists in taking off and putting on his greasy cap ; a prima donna, who goes yawning, drawling, twaddling through her mumbled part, with eyes well open to the chance of selling her overblown charms in quite another market than the theatre. The show is seasoned with loathsome buffooneries and interludes which ought to send their performers to the galleys.

These profane comedians pervert the noble use of their ancient art by presenting nothing which is not openly disreputable and scandalous. The filth which falls continually from their lips infects themselves and their profession with the foulest infamy. They are less civil than donkeys in their action, no better than pimps and ruffians in their gestures, equal to public prostitutes in their immodesty of speech. Knavery and lewdness inspire all their motions. In everything they stink of impudicity and villainy. When occasions offer for veiling grossness under a cloak of decorum, they

[1] *Op. cit.*, Vol. I., p. 73

HARLEQUIN'S BOW

From the engraving after Claude Gillot (1673–1722)

do not take these, but pique themselves on bringing beastliness to sight by barefaced bawdry and undisguised indecency.

In the case of reputable actors the use of masks and the circumscribed *rôles* of the characters tended to become stereotyped and monotonous. After years of hard wear the repertory of jokes and " business " had become threadbare and worn out. While the actors were artists, their spontaneity of gesture and the lively invention of their dialogue concealed in some measure these shortcomings. But the movement had lost its appeal and received its death blow from the pen of Carlo Goldoni, who substituted witty, written comedies based on the life of the people. Goldoni's attitude towards the Masks is summed up in his preface [1] to the Pasquali edition (1761) of his plays : " The comic theatre of Italy for more than a century past had so degenerated that it became a disgusting object of general abhorrence. You saw nothing on public stages but indecent harlequinades, dirty and scandalous intrigue, foul jests, immodest loves. Plots were badly constructed, and worse carried out in action, without order, without propriety of manners. . . . People of culture, nay, the common folk, cried out against these miserable travesties. Every one was wearied with the insipidities and conventionalities of an art upon the wane. You knew what Harlequin or Pantaloon was going to say before he opened his lips."

Carlo Gozzi championed the cause of the masks by writing for their use his brilliantly satirical *Fiabe*. But the first brief success of these pieces depended more on music, elaborate scenery and effects, and sumptuous spectacle than on the improvised humour of the buffoons. For a few years the balance swayed to and fro, but Goldoni triumphed, and Harlequin and his kindred disappeared from the theatre, from the temporary stage, from the market-place, to linger in effigy in the nomad puppet-shows which still may be encountered amid the scenes of their greatest triumphs when they were alive and a vital force in the theatre.

[1] Quoted Symonds, *op. cit.*, Vol. I., p. 72.

Chapter Nine

Harlequin in England

IT is time to relate the history of Harlequin in England. There is no doubt but that the early Elizabethan drama owed something of its structure and plots to the Italian theatre, but, as Dr. Smith[1] has pointed out, this was due rather to personal intercourse between the actors of the two nationalities than through the medium of printed texts. Not only did Italian players visit England, playing both at court and in the city, but English companies played abroad, often concurrently with Italian actors, at Vienna, Paris, and throughout Spain. Heywood declares : " The cardinall at Bruxels hath at this time in pay a company of our English comedians. The French king allowes certaine companies in Paris, Orleans, besides other cities : so doth the king of Spaine, in Civill, Madrill, and other provinces." [2] Nash, who was possibly a member of one of these companies, describes a meeting he had, while on his travels, with an Italian player :

Comming from Venice the last Summer, and taking Bergamo in my waye homeward to England, it was my happe, souiourning there foure or fiue dayes, to light in felowship with that famous Francatrip' [3] Harlicken, who,

---

[1] *Op. cit.*, p. 170.

[2] *Apology for Actors* (Shakespeare Soc.), 1841, p. 60.

[3] *Franca Trippa :* a name given to a Zanni Mask created by Gabriele Panzanini. See Rasi, *op. cit.*, Vol. II., pp. 212, 213, for an account of this player, and *cf.* Callot, *I Balli di Sfessania* (?1622).

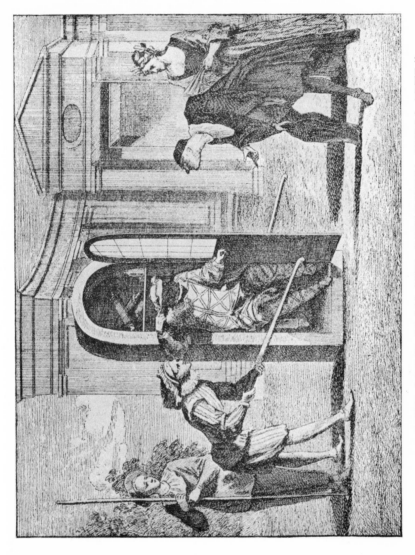

HARLEQUIN SCENE FROM THE " COMMEDIA DELL' ARTE "

From the engraving after Claude Gillot

perceiuing me to bee an English man by my habit and speech, asked me
many particulars of the order and maner of our playes, which he termed by
the name of representations : amongst other talke he enquired of me if I
knew any such Parabolano here in London as Signior Chiarlatano Kempino.
Very well, (quoth I,) and haue beene oft in his company. He, hearing me say
so, began to embrace me a new, and offered me all the courtesie he colde for
his sake, saying, although he knew him not, yet for the report he had hard of
his pleasance, hee colde not but bee in loue with his perfections being
absent.[1]

The *Revels Accounts* for 1573 contain references to performances given by " the Italyan players " and expenses incurred in connection with them. For example, between February and November
of that year, payments were made " ffor the Progresse to Reading
&c. And Lykewize ffor the Ayringes, Repayrings, Translatinges,
preparing, ffytting, ffurnishing, Garnishing, Attending, and setting
foorth, of sundry kyndes of Apparell propertyes and ffurnyture for
the Italyan players that ffollowed the progresse and made pastyme
fyrst at Wynsor and afterwardes at Reading." The charges include
the following articles : " A plank of ffyrr & other pieces of sawen
wood. Golde Lether for cronetes. Thred & sheperdes hookes.
Lamskynnes for Shepperds. Horstayles for the wylde mannes
garment. Arrowes for Nymphes. Lightes and shepperdes staves.
Hoopes for Garlandes. Baye Leaves and flowers. The hyer of A
Syth for Saturne." [2]

Laneham, describing the Kenilworth festivities in 1575, says :

Noow within allso . . . waz thear sheawed before her Highness by an
Italian, such feats of agilitie, in goinges, turninges, tumblinges, castinges,
hops, jumps, leaps, skips, springs, gambaud, soomersauts, caprettiez and
flights ; forward, backward, sydewize, a downward, upward, and with
sundry windings, gyrings and circumflexions ; allso lightly and with such
easiness, as by me in feaw words it iz not expressibl by pen or speech, I tell
yoo plain. I bleast me by my faith to behold him, and began to doout whither
a waz a man or a sprite. . . . Az for thiz fellow, I cannot tell what to make

---

[1] *An Almond for a Parrat*, 1590. Included in *The Works of Thomas Nashe*,
Edit. by R. B. McKerrow, 5 Vols., 1905. Vol. III., p. 342.
[2] Feuillerat (A.), *Documents relating to the Office of the Revels in the Time of
Queen Elizabeth*. 1908, pp. 225, 227, 228.

of him, save that I may gesse hiz bak be metalld like a lamprey, that haz no bone, but a lyne like a lute-string.[1]

On the 13th of January, 1577, the Privy Council directed " the Lord Maiour of London to geve order that one Dronsiano, an Italian, a commediante and his companye may playe within the Cittie and the Liberties of the same betweene this and the firste weeke in Lent." [2] It is generally accepted that the Dronsiano mentioned was Drusiano Martinelli, brother of the celebrated Harlequin Tristano Martinelli.

There is abundant evidence that the Italian Masks were well known to the authors of the period. Thomas Heywood speaks of " all the doctors, zawnyes, pantaloones, harlakeenes, in which the French, but especially the Italians, have beene excellent." [3] Shakespeare, in his comedy *As You Like It*, likens the sixth age of man to

> . . . the lean and slipper'd pantaloon
> With spectacles on nose, and pouch on side.

Marston, in the *Malcontent*, refers to " the French Harlakene." Day, in his *Ile of Gulls*, has : " I, like a Harlakene in an Italian comedy, stand making faces at both their follies." In Jonson's *Every Man in His Humour* a character says : " He's like a zany to a tumbler that tries tricks after him to make men laugh." Kyd, in his *Spanish Tragedy*, remarks :

> The Italian tragedians were so sharp of wit
> That in one hour's meditation
> They would perform anything in action.

And these are but a tithe of the references that could be cited.

Another, though very questionable, proof of the influence of Italian technique on English actors may exist in the discovery made by Edmond Malone in Dulwich College. Among the memoranda left by the theatrical manager Henslowe and his son-in-law the

[1] Nichols, *op. cit.*, Vol. I., pp. 440–1.
[2] *Acts of the Privy Council of England*. New Series. Edit. by J. R. Dasent, Vol. X. (1577–1578), 1895, p. 144.
[3] *Op. cit.*, p. 43.

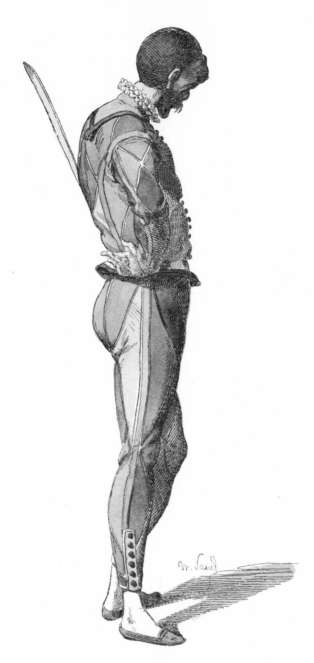

FRENCH HARLEQUIN (1858)

From Sand's " Masques et Buffons "

actor Edward Alleyn, Malone found four cardboard tables on each of which the plot of a play was set down, in two columns, together with the names of the characters, their exits and entrances, cues for music and so forth. Each card had a square hole at the top of it, obviously so that it could be hung up on a peg behind the stage, as were the *scenari* used by the Italian comedians. But, beyond pointing out that the *Commedia dell' Arte* influenced to some extent early English drama, it is well not to ascribe too much importance to it ; again, it is unlikely that the English actor generally was gifted with that facility of improvisation possessed by the Italian players.

A " harlekin " is a character in the 4th Entry in *Britannia Triumphans*, a Masque by Inigo Jones and Sir W. D'Avenant presented at Whitehall before Charles I. on the Sunday after Twelfth Night, 1637. With the advent of the Civil War and the establishment of the Commonwealth the theatre was suppressed by Parliament. But the return of the pleasure-loving Charles II. raised the ban and gave a new impetus to this popular form of entertainment.

The first performance of Harlequin in a theatre was that given by Joe Haines in 1667, who played the part in Ravenscroft's *Scaramouche a Philosopher, Harlequin a Schoolboy, Bravo, Merchant & Magician, a comedy after the Italian manner*. Harlequin next appears in *The Emperor of the Moon*, a farce written by Mrs. Aphra Behn. Lowe says of this play, " One of the best pantomimic farces ever seen." It was first produced in 1687, with Tom Jevon as Harlequin, who made a great success in the part, at the Duke's Theatre, Dorset Gardens. Jevon also acted Harlequin in Mountford's *Dr. Faustus*, given in 1685 (?). Harlequin appears in another of Mrs. Behn's plays, *The Rover* (Part II.), *or The Banish'd Cavaliers*, produced in 1697.

About this time dancing or tumbling Harlequins became a great feature of the London fairs, while the theatres began to engage the French *forains*.[1] There was strenuous competition between the two

[1] Players in the *Théâtres de la Foire*, that is, players who set up their theatres and booths at public fairs.

English companies, and the actors sought to draw their public with raree-shows rather than permit them to go and see their rival's plays. Rowe, in his epilogue to *The Ambitious Stepmother*, produced at Lincoln's Inn Fields in 1700, complains :

> Show but a mimic ape, or French buffoon,
> You to the other house in shoals are gone,
> And leave us here to tune our crowds alone.
> Must Shakespear, Fletcher and laborious Ben,
> Be left for Scaramouche and Harlequin ?

During the season 1701–2 the Sieurs Alard presented *An Italian Night Scene* at Drury Lane. It is difficult to state with accuracy when the first pantomime proper was shown on the English stage. Weaver asserts that " the first entertainment that appeared on the English Stage, where the Representation and Story was carried on by Dancing, Action and Motion only, was performed in Grotesque Characters, after the manner of the Modern Italians, such as Harlequin, Scaramouch, &c., and was called The Tavern Bilkers. Composed by Mr. Weaver And first performed in Drury Lane Theatre, 1702." [1] We have, however, been unable to discover proof of this statement ; we cannot find any playbill, or any advertisement in the *Daily Courant*, announcing the production of this piece. Mr. Disher [2] has pointed out that actually Weaver was at Lincoln's Inn Fields in that year, and the law forbidding actors to transfer their services had just been reinforced. Hence we are inclined to doubt Weaver's statement, the more so in that it was not made until 1728, and the evidence indicates a date posterior to 1702.

By 1715, Harlequin, Pulcinella and Scaramouch had become so popular that plays were frequently followed by dances in which players dressed in the traditional costume of these Masks figured prominently. The files of the *Daily Courant* have many references to these entertainments. At Lincoln's Inn Fields on the 18th of

[1] *The History of Mimes and Pantomimes*, 1728, p. 43.
[2] *Clowns and Pantomimes*, 1925, p. 229.

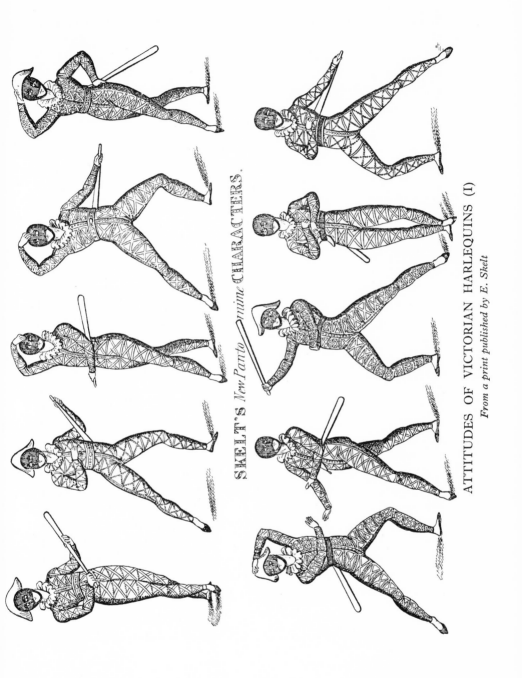

SKELT'S *New Panto*~*mime* CHARACTERS.

ATTITUDES OF VICTORIAN HARLEQUINS (I)

From a print published by E. Skelt

April there was a " Dance of two Scaramouches," " An Entertainment between a Harlequin and Two Punches," and on the 23rd of April an " Entertainment betwixt a Countryman and a Harlequin." In November there was an " Italian Night-scene between a Harlequin, a Scaramouche and a Punchinello." In April, 1716, M. Sorin and Mr. Baxter, " lately arrived from Paris," presented Harlequin and Scaramouch at Drury Lane in such plays as *The Whimsical Death of Harlequin*, and *La Guinguette, or Harlequin Turned Tapster*.

The actor-manager John Rich was the first to establish pantomime on a firm footing. In the *Daily Courant* for the 20th of December, 1717, he advertises an Italian Mimic Scene (as he called his pantomimes) entitled *Harlequin Executed : A new Italian Mimic Scene between a Scaramouch, a Harlequin, a Country Farmer, his Wife and others*. Rich's first great success was *The Necromancer, or, History of Dr. Faustus*.

In general, these pantomimes were divided into two parts, one serious and one comic. There was the lover story of Harlequin and Columbine, in the course of which Harlequin effected, by the aid of his wand, the most wonderful transformations and enchantments. Not a little of the success of Rich's pantomimes was due to the ingenious manner in which he combined the ideas of conjuring and transformation. Davies has left us an excellent account of what a Rich pantomime was like :

It consisted of two parts, one serious, and the other comic. By the help of gay scenes, fine habits, grand dances, appropriate music, and other decorations, he exhibited a story from Ovid's Metamorphoses, or some other fabulous writer. Between the pauses or acts of this serious representation he interwove a comic fable, consisting chiefly of the courtship of Harlequin and Columbine, with a variety of surprising adventures and tricks, which were produced by the magic wand of Harlequin ; such as the sudden transformation of palaces and temples to huts and cottages ; of men and women into wheel-barrows and joint-stools ; of trees turned to houses ; colonnades to beds of tulips ; and mechanic shops into serpents and ostriches.[1]

[1] *Memoirs of the Life of David Garrick*, 2 Vols., 1808, Vol. I., p. 130.

The novelist Henry Fielding also gives an interesting, if antagonistic, account of a pantomime :

This entertainment consisted of two parts, which the inventor distinguished by the names of the serious and comic. The serious exhibits a certain number of heathen gods and goddesses who were certainly the worst and dullest company into which an audience was ever introduced ; and (which was a secret known to few) were actually intended so to be in order to contrast the comic part of the entertainment and to display the tricks of Harlequin to the better advantage. And this will now plainly appear if instead of serious and comic we supply the words duller and dullest ; for the comic was certainly duller than anything before shown on the stage.[1]

Nevertheless, when the evidence is sifted, it is clear that Rich, both as producer and mime, achieved a very considerable success.

The rival managers of the playhouses regarded with extreme disfavour the success of the novelty, Cibber remarking : " The lower, in Reputation, has always been forc'd to exhibit some new-fangled Foppery, to draw the Multitude after them." [2] As a counter to the increasing success of pantomime, there was printed in 1724 an unsigned pamphlet, entitled *The British Stage ; or, The Exploits of Harlequin : a Farce, designed as an After Entertainment for the Audiences of Harlequin Doctor Faustus and the Necromancer.* Here is a verse and a quotation from the work :

> Here you've a Dragon, Windmill, and a Devil,
> A Doctor, Conjurer ; all wondrous civil ;
> A Harlequin, and Puppets, Ghosts and Fiends,
> And Raree-Show to gain some Actors Ends ;
> So perfectly polite is grown this Town
> No Play, without a Windmill, will go down.

I frequently bit my lips whilst others were laughing, and often laugh'd when others were silent . . . met with far greater applause than the Politest and most Elegant Play that ever appeared upon the British Theatre.

But presently the other managers began to imitate Rich's example. Cibber excuses himself thus : " I did it against my con-

---

[1] *Tom Jones*, Book V., chap. 1.
[2] *An Apology for the Life of Mr. Colley Cibber*, 4th Edit., 1740, p. 299.

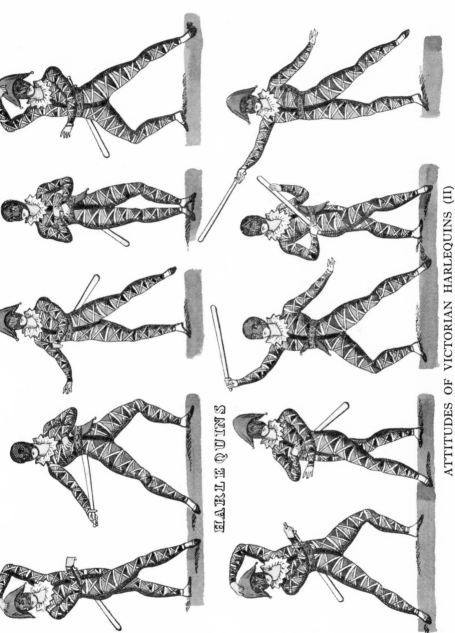

HARLEQUINS

ATTITUDES OF VICTORIAN HARLEQUINS (II)

From a print published by E. Skelt

science and had not virtue enough to starve, by opposing a multitude, that would have been too hard for me." [1]

In 1734, a pantomime, *Mars and Venus*, was produced at Drury Lane, and another, *Dr. Faustus*, a favourite subject, in which figured Macklin, Theo. Cibber, Mrs. Clive and Mrs. Cibber. There is a change of tone in the criticisms, for of the latter a contemporary observes : " Happy is it that we live in an age of taste, when the dumb elegance and natural wit and humour of Harlequin are justly preferred to the whining of Tragedy, or the vulgarity of Comedy." Pantomime achieved an ever-increasing vogue. Even the great actor Garrick, finding his audiences at Drury Lane dwindling to nothing, remarked : " If you won't come to *Lear* or *Hamlet*, I must give you Harlequin." His Harlequin was Woodward, said to have been surpassed by Rich alone. The craze for pantomime lasted right on to the second half of the nineteenth century, and an examination of the programmes of performances given over this period reveals the startling fact that managers presenting even great actors in great plays, like those of Shakespeare, almost invariably baited their bills with a harlequinade.

In 1739, Rich produced at Covent Garden the pantomime *Orpheus and Eurydice*. Rich was the Harlequin, Happerly the Clown and Signor Pietro Grimaldi the Pantaloon. Occasionally Signor Grimaldi played Harlequin. Rich died in 1761, and in the same year a determined effort was made to deal a death-blow to the seemingly immortal character of Harlequin. The authors, Murphy and Foote, devised a play, entitled *The Wishes*, which ridiculed Harlequin, a pasteboard effigy being hung in full view of the audience. But the public refused to have their idol maligned. A tremendous uproar ensued, and it was necessary to announce the play at an end.

Another blow at pantomime was dealt by Churchill in *The Rosciad* (1761) :

> HARLEQUIN comes their chief !—see from afar,
> The hero seated in fantastic car !

[1] *Op. cit.*, p. 300.

Wedded to *Novelty*, his only arms
Are wooden swords, wands, talismans, and charms ;
On one side Folly sits, by some call'd Fun,
And on the other, his arch-patron, Lun.
Behind, for liberty a-thirst in vain,
Sense, helpless captive, drags the galling chain.
Six rude mis-shapen beasts the chariot draw,
Whom Reason loaths, and Nature never saw,
Monsters, with tails of ice, and heads of fire ;
Gorgons, and Hydras, and Chymaeras dire.
Each was bestrode by full as monstrous wight,
Giant, Dwarf, Genius, Elf, Hermaphrodite.
The Town, as usual, met him in full cry ;
The Town, as usual, knew no reason why.
But Fashion so directs, and Moderns raise
On Fashion's mould'ring base their transient praise.[1]

On the 19th of September, 1764, Signor Grimaldi had his benefit at Sadler's Wells. Included in the programme was *A New Entertainment of Music and Dancing called Don Quixote.* The Harlequin was Mr. Banks. At Drury Lane, on the 26th of December of the same year, *Queen Mab* was produced, the Harlequin being played by Mr. Rooker, the Pantaloon by Signor Grimaldi. On the 18th of December, 1779, Signor Grimaldi was presented with a son, Joseph, who was to become the most famous Clown in the history of the British stage.

About this time it would appear that pantomime had deteriorated, for on the 3rd of November, 1782, Walpole, writing to the Countess of Ossory, remarks of a pantomime he had just visited : " How unlike the pantomimes of Rich, which were full of wit, and coherent, and carried on a story. What I now saw was *Robinson Crusoe :* how Aristotle and Bossu, had they ever written on pantomimes, would swear ! It was a heap of contradictions and violations of the costume. *Friday* is turned into Harlequin, and falls down at an old man's feet that I took for Pantaloon, but they told me that it was *Friday's* father. I said, ' Then it must be

[1] 9th Edit., 1765, p. 32.

92

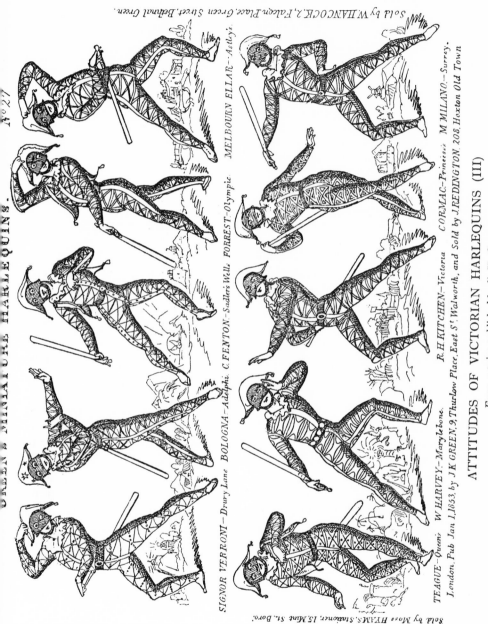

SIGNOR VERRONI—Drury Lane. BOLOGNA—Adelphi. C. FENTON—Sadlers Wells. FORREST—Olympic. MELBOURN ELLAR—Astley's.

R.H.KITCHEN—Victoria. CORMAC—Princess's. M.MILANO—Surrey.

TEAGUE—Queens. W.HARVEY—Marylebone.

London. Pub Jan 1.1853, by J.K.GREEN, 9, Thurlow Place, East Sᵗ Walworth, and Sold by J.REDINGTON 208, Hoxton Old Town.

Sold by W.HANCOCK, 2, Falcon Place, Green Street, Bethnal Green.

Sold by Moss HYAMS, Stationer, 15, Mint St, Boro'.

ATTITUDES OF VICTORIAN HARLEQUINS (III)

From a print published by J. K. Green

Thursday,' yet still it seemed to be Pantaloon. I see I understand nothing from astronomy to a harlequin-farce ! " [1]

In the final quarter of the century pantomime-writers took their plots from old ballads and fairy tales, and in the last years from popular books on travel. A good specimen of the latter type is *Harlequin Teague, or, The Giant's Causeway*, produced in 1782 at the Haymarket. This is particularly interesting in that it was the first pantomime to create Harlequin by metamorphosis.

Some ten years later another novelty was introduced in the pantomime *Robin Hood, or Merry Sherwood*, in which Harlequin appeared without a Columbine. On the 29th of December, 1806, the most famous of pantomimes, *Harlequin and Mother Goose, or, The Golden Egg*, by Thomas Dibdin, was produced at Covent Garden. The great success [2] of this piece was due mainly to the extraordinary variety and ingenuity of its trick scenes, for it had neither gorgeous processions, nor splendid banners, nor expensive scenery ; Harlequin would have had to forego his spangles even but for Grimaldi's advice. The Harlequin was doubled by Mr. King and Mr. Bologna, Jun.

In order to convey some idea of what the pantomimes were like at this period we reproduce Planché's description :

A pretty story—a nursery tale—dramatically told, in which " the course of true love never did run smooth," formed the opening ; the characters being a cross-grained old father, with a pretty daughter who had two suitors —one a poor young fellow, whom she preferred, the other a wealthy fop, whose pretensions were of course favoured by the father. There was also a body-servant of some sort in the old man's establishment. At the moment when the young lady was about to be forcibly married to the fop she despised, or on the point of eloping with the youth of her choice, the good Fairy made her appearance, and, changing the refractory pair into Harlequin and Columbine, the old curmudgeon into Pantaloon, and the body-servant into Clown, the two latter, in company with the rejected Lover, as he was called, commenced the pursuit of the happy pair, and the comic business consisted of a dozen or more cleverly constructed scenes, in which all the tricks and changes

---

[1] *The Letters of Horace Walpole, Earl of Oxford*. Edit. by P. Cunningham. 9 Vols. 1858. Vol. VIII., pp. 296, 297.
[2] It ran for ninety-two nights.

had a meaning, and were introduced as contrivances to favour the escape of Harlequin and Columbine, when too closely followed by their enemies. There was as regular a plot as might be found in a melodrama. An interest in the chase increased the admiration of the ingenuity and the enjoyment of the fun of the tricks by which the runaways escaped capture, till the inevitable " dark scene " came—a cavern or a forest in which they were overtaken, seized, and the Magic Wand which had so uniformly aided them snatched from the grasp of the despairing Harlequin, and flourished in triumph by the Clown. Again at the critical moment the protecting Fairy appeared, and, exacting the consent of the father to the marriage of the devoted couple, transported the whole party to what was really a grand last scene, which everybody did wait for.[1]

During the eighteenth century there had been isolated speaking-pantomimes, such as Garrick's *Harlequin's Invasion*, followed in the succeeding century by further examples like *Doctor Hocus-Pocus, or, Harlequin Washed White* (1814), and Planché's *Rodolph the Wolf, or, Little Red Riding Hood*, given on the 21st of December, 1818, at the Olympic Pavilion. Opening scenes were sung until 1830, when Mark Lemon wrote a burlesque to precede the harlequinade in *Harlequin Fat and Harlequin Bat, or, The Giant's Causeway*, produced at Covent Garden. Planché says of this device :

Where harlequinades were indispensable at Christmas, the ingenious method was hit upon of dovetailing extravaganza and pantomime. Instead of the two or three simple scenes which previously formed the opening of the pantomime, a long burlesque, the characters in which have nothing to do with those in the harlequinade, occupies an hour—sometimes much more— of the evening, and terminates with one of those elaborate and gorgeous displays which have acquired the name of " transformation scenes," and are made the great feature of the evening ; and, consequently, after which the best part of the audience quit the theatre, and what is by courtesy called the " comic business " is run through by the pantomimists in three or four ordinary street or chamber scenes. The usual number of curiously dressed people stream in and out of exhibitions or cross the stage ; the usual number of policemen are bonneted ; the steps are buttered ; the red-hot poker is exhibited ; the real live pig let out of the basket ; and then, *à propos de bottes*, a portion of the transformation scene is suddenly discovered, sufficiently shorn of its beams to escape recognition by the two or three score of

[1] *Recollections and Reflections*, Rev. Edit., 1901, p. 339.

MR HONOR AS HARLEQUIN.

From a print in the collection of H. J. Webb

persons who have courageously sat out the performance, and are too much occupied in putting on their coats and shawls to think of anything but their beds or their suppers. The " transformation scene " is, however, declared every year to be unparalleled. That is the object of attraction, and all the rest is " inexplicable dumb show and noise." [1]

" Joe," as the great Grimaldi was called familiarly, made his first appearance at the age of three at Sadler's Wells. At Christmas in the same year he appeared at Drury Lane in *Harlequin Junior, or, The Magic Cestus*. It is not within the scope of this volume to follow Grimaldi through his many triumphs, and the great number of pantomimes with which he made himself inseparably associated, until his retirement on the 17th of March, 1828. Among the Harlequins who worked with him, at one time or another, were Jack Bologna, James Byrne, Tom Ellar,[2] Guerint, Hartland, King, Ridgway,[3] C. J. Smith and Sutton. Other Harlequins of the first half of the nineteenth century were Aird, Cormac, Deulin, M. Ellar, C. Fenton, Forrest, French, W. Harvey, Hope, Howell, R. H. Kitchin, Nelson Lee, Lewis Polworth and Taylor. Publishers of theatrical prints, and scenes and characters for model theatres, such as Bailey, Hodgson, Jameson, Redington, Skelt, Webb and West, have left us portraits in character of these artistes, many of which, however, are facially so much alike as to render questionable the accuracy of their resemblance. Other Harlequins have tripped in their wake, but none of especial importance.

Grimaldi died on the 31st of May, 1837. Much of the continued vogue and success of the harlequinade was due to the excellent mime, humour and comic " business " which he provided so lavishly in his performances. And his supreme talent made the Clown the most important figure in the entertainment. He became the pivot on which everything turned. Harlequin, once the prime actor as conceived by Rich, began to share his importance with Columbine, Pantaloon and the Clown. Soon the Clown was the

---

[1] *Op. cit.*, p. 338.
[2] Also written " Eller."
[3] Ridgway made his first appearance as Harlequin in *Jan Ben Jan, or, Harlequin and the Forty Virgins*, produced at Sadler's Wells on the 30th of March, 1807.

centre of interest, and the character of Harlequin accordingly dwindled into insignificance. Another contributory cause to Harlequin's decline was the passion for raree-shows. Thomas Dibdin's *Harlequin Hoax ; or, A Pantomime Proposed : A Comic Extravaganza*, contains the following dialogue :

PATCH. Now, Sir, I want to introduce my *hero* at this part of the Pantomime.

MANAGER. You *have* introduced him ; isn't Harlequin the hero ?

PATCH. Bless your unpractised head ! Harlequin ! no ; he's only the agent of another. Who thinks of Harlequin, while there's a chimpanzee, a bear, a rein-deer, a cat, or a goose to be had ? I must have something that will *strike*—something that will make a noise in the world. I'll have a grand necromantic lover, disguised like—like a lion.[1]

Soon after Grimaldi's death extravaganzas became the vogue. These relied for their success on costliness of production and magnificence of scenery rather than on the skill of the performers. Transformation scenes, glittering with gold and silver leaf and scintillating with mica, with their myriad fairies grouped on the stage and suspended in the air by wires from the " flies," were introduced and developed at enormous expense. The harlequinades were cut shorter and shorter until they were little more than an epilogue, or dessert, to the feast of light and colour that had gone before. And when the Clown was hard put to it to set a foot upon the stage, poor Harlequin could scarce show his face. His mask had become so potent that he was well-nigh invisible to the audience !

And how strange this is, for there never has been a more popular theatrical character than Harlequin. In one guise or another he has appeared on every European stage ; the plays and dances in which he has figured must run into hundreds. Here are some of the printed plays in English : *Harlequin a Sorcerer*, 1725 ; *Harlequin, Prince in a Dream*, 1726 ; *Harlequin Misfortune*, 1726 ; *Harlequin Student*, 1741 ; *Harlequin Incendiary*, 1746 ; *Harlequin Mungo*, 1750 ; *Harlequin Premier*, 1769 ; *Harlequin's Trip to*

[1] *Harlequin Hoax*, 1814, p. 19.

MR ELLAR AS HARLEQUIN

From a print in the collection of H. J. Webb

Naples, 1772 ; *The Choice of Harlequin*, 1782 ; *Harlequin's Chaplet*,
1790 ; *Harlequin Wanderer*, 1792 ; *Harlequin's Museum*, 1793 ;
Harlequin Made Happy, 1796 ; *Harlequin's Tormentors*, 1797 ;
Harlequin Quixotte, 1797 ; *Harlequin's Amulet*, 1801 ; *A Description of Harlequin in his Element*, 1810 ; *New Pantomime of Harlequin and Fortunio*, 1815 ; *Harlequin and the Eagle*, 1826.

An interesting book entitled *The History and Comical Adventures of Harlequin, and his Pleasing Companion Columbine*, was
published in 1790. The story concerns the adventures of a poor
boy who witnessed a puppet-show and was so delighted with the
antics of Harlequin that he aspired to imitate him. He gains
employment and is permitted by his master to go to Sadler's Wells
Theatre, where he forms acquaintance with the actors and finally
becomes a Harlequin. There is another book, by Stirling Coyne,
published in 1886, with the alluring title *Sam Spangles, or, The
History of Harlequin*, but, alas, on perusal, it proves to be a very dull
performance.

At the beginning of the second half of the nineteenth century
Harlequin was sometimes played by women, from which practice
the " principal boy " is said to have originated. A very entertaining
but now almost forgotten book affords an excellent idea of the
manner of production of a pantomime of the " sixties." First, let
us observe Harlequin at rehearsal :

A flexible tube conveys gas to an upright in the orchestra, where sits the
leader of the ballet music looking over and trying his grand overture to the
forthcoming Christmas novelty, while a *répétiteur* is busy scraping away at
the Elfin Waltz, which a lady and gentleman, curiously attired, are practising
on the stage. The lady is dressed in an old pair of silk tights, dirty satin
shoes, worn-out ballet skirt, a felt bonnet, and a warm cloth polka. " Is it
possible ! " exclaim our young friends ; " can that be columbine ? And is
that really harlequin ? " " Yes," we reply, " that is the doomed princess,
afterwards columbine ; and her companion in the white trousers, pea-coat,
and buff shoes, is the knight of the spangles—harlequin." These are their
working clothes they have on ; but wait till boxing-night, and what couple
will be more resplendent.[1]

[1] *Glimpses of Real Life as seen in the Theatrical World and in Bohemia : Being the
Confessions of Peter Paterson, a Strolling Comedian.* Edinburgh, 1864, pp. 265, 266.

From the same source we learn that the Clown was responsible for the planning of the " comic business," that is, the fun and frolic which succeeded the transformation scene. His directions were set down on paper with, apparently, more regard for effect than for spelling and grammar :

PROGRAM OF COMIC BUISNES

IN THE PANTOMIME

A cascaid at the fall of the Curtain by the caracturs ;

(*i.e., after the transformation scene*).

Scene First.—Pcultry shop and Tailor shop—set.

Dance by Harlequin and Columbine ; then sprites to cross and Recross.

Rabits and poultry on The stall with very larg Goos.

BUISNES.

Enter Clown and Pantaloon steeling goos (buisnes) enter tax colecktor with larg sumonds (writ) writen on it assecesed tax, then buisnes with the tailor, when he exits boy with pie. Buis : Tax colecktor police and tailor and old woman (spill).[1]

The characters in the harlequinade would make a most effective scene out of such a plan, which, to the uninitiated, seems the vaguest outline. Dickens, in an article contributed to *The Theatre*, urges actors and actresses to study the gestures and attitudes of Harlequin :

A few lessons in the business of Harlequin would teach many a young man, for instance, the simple lesson that arms may be moved with advantage from the shoulder as well as from the elbow ; and so we should get rid of one of the awkwardest, ugliest, and commonest stage tricks. And there would be nothing derogatory in the study. Many of our most distinguished actors have graduated in Pantomime.

How many of us in our childhood have spent the evening of Boxing Day at Drury Lane to enjoy again the ever youthful histories of *Aladdin, Cinderella, Puss in Boots,* or *Dick Whittington*— now little more than vehicles for music-hall " gags " and topical allusions ! At eleven o'clock the curtain falls on the pantomime.

---

[1] *Op. cit.,* p. 273.

Mr HOWARD LEWIS as HARLEQUIN

Publish'd by M. SKELT, No 11, Swan Street, Minories, London

From a print in the collection of H. J. Webb

A shrill whistle, and the curtain rises on a street scene with shops, the walls plastered thickly with glaring advertisements of local tradesmen. Enter Clown, Harlequin, Pantaloon and Columbine. A gigantic Christmas cracker is brought upon the stage and pulled by Clown and Pantaloon. Precious seconds are wasted in throwing the contents, small crackers, to the audience. The Clown steals some sausages from a butcher's shop . . . burns a policeman with a red-hot poker . . . assaults Pantaloon to reproachful cries of " Oh, Joey ! " . . . Meanwhile Harlequin and Columbine meander to and fro with an occasional pirouette. Already people are rudely rising from their seats to pull on their coats and button their gloves. The curtain falls. It is the pall of Pantomime, the shroud of Harlequin.

Chapter Ten

Some English Harlequins

ONE of the earliest English Harlequins was Tom Jevon, born in 1652, an actor of low comedy parts, who played this character in Mrs. Behn's *The Empress of the Moon*, produced at the Queen's Theatre in 1687. Much of the plot was borrowed from the celebrated piece *Arlequin Empereur dans la Lune*, and much of the " business," such as the scene in the first act, where Harlequin tries to commit suicide, first by stopping up his mouth and nose with his hands and then by tickling himself, was derived from the same source. A contemporary says that Jevon, " young, slim and most graceful of dancers, proved himself the King of Harlequins, past, present and to come." Thus the English Harlequin, like his Italian ancestor, excelled in dancing. This is easily explained in Jevon's case, for he began life as a dancing-master. Jevon also tried his hand at play-writing; he was the author of *The Devil of a Wife, or, A Comical Transformation*, produced at Dorset Gardens in 1686. He died in 1688 and was buried at Hampstead.

The Emperor of the Moon was revived in 1702, when the part of Harlequin was taken by the actor William Penkethman. On the 18th of September this player appeared without his mask, a novelty which had disastrous effect on his performance. Colley Cibber gives an interesting account of this incident :

M.ʳ AULD.

From a print published by W. West, in the British Museum

When he (Penkethman) first play'd *Harlequin* in the *Emperor* of the *Moon*, several Gentlemen (who inadvertently judg'd by the Rules of Nature) fancy'd that a great deal of the Drollery, and Spirit of his Grimace was lost, by his wearing that useless, unmeaning Masque of a black Cat, and therefore insisted, that the next time of his acting that Part, he should play without it : Their desire was accordingly comply'd with—but, alas ! in vain—*Penkethman* could not take to himself the Shame of the Character without being conceal'd—he was no more *Harlequin*—his Humour was quite disconcerted ! his Conscience could not with the same *Effronterie* declare against Nature, without the Cover of that unchanging Face, which he was sure would never blush for it ! no ! it was quite another Case ! without that Armour his Courage could not come up to the bold Strokes, that were necessary to get the better of common Sense.[1]

The next and perhaps the most important of English Harlequins was the actor-manager John Rich, whose great work in the establishment of pantomime has been briefly reviewed. He was born about the year 1692 and was the son of Christopher Rich, the one time patentee of Drury Lane Theatre. The father sought to capture the town with exhibitions of French dancers, Italian singers and other exotic forms of entertainment. His son inherited the same singular taste. On coming into possession of the Lincoln's Inn Fields Theatre, left to him by his father, he determined to indulge his passion for tragic parts. On the 18th of December, 1714, he declaimed the prologue to Farquhar's *The Recruiting Officer*, and in 1715 made his first appearance in the title *rôle* of *Unhappy Favourite, or, The Earl of Essex*, by T. J. Banks. His efforts being coldly received by the public, he turned his thoughts to the presentation of pantomime, a form of entertainment then little known in this country, save for Weaver's experiments, and, for that matter, hardly attempted abroad. Pantomime differed from the representations of the Improvised Comedy in that the harlequinade characters, Harlequin, Clown, Pantaloon and Columbine, performed entirely in dumb show, while the Italian comedians mimed, spoke and sang.

There is an interesting half-length portrait [2] of Rich in private

[1] *Op. cit.*, pp. 90, 91.
[2] The painting in the possession of His Honour Judge Wood. A reproduction

dress which presents him as a middle-aged man with plump, rubicund features, a slight double chin, and humorous eyes and mouth. He looks very much the country squire of the period, enjoying rude health and fond of the pleasures of the table.

Rich suffered from a neglected education ; and though he wrote well, his speech was vulgar and ungrammatical. He spoke of " larning " Wilkinson [1] to be a player, told Signora Spiletto to lay the emphasis on the " adjutant " and said " turbot " for turban. But his business acumen and flair for dramatic talent enabled him to keep his theatre open, despite the rival attractions of Garrick, then at the height of his fame.

Jackson relates several anecdotes of the whimsical actor-manager, of which the following will serve as an example :

A candidate for the buskin, being desired to repeat the celebrated soliloquy in Hamlet, began, to-be, or not to-be. Rich very gravely replied, " Toby may be a very good dog, Mister, but Toby will not do for me. You need not therefore trouble yourself any farther, Mister." [2]

Rich excelled in at least five branches of his profession ; as a manager, as a contriver of pantomimes, as a designer of the mechanical devices necessary to produce the illusions he required, as a mime in the character of Harlequin, and as a teacher of actors their business.

A consideration of the reception of his pantomimes produced at Lincoln's Inn Fields and Covent Garden Theatres from 1717 to 1761 reveals the fact that hardly one failed to please, and there were few that did not run for forty or fifty nights. Rich himself played Harlequin under the stage name of Lun, and as a mime was undoubtedly quite exceptional. A Scene with a Statue and another called *Catching a Butterfly* were particularly associated with him. Jackson says of his appearance in *Harlequin Sorcerer*,[3]

of this forms the frontispiece to Wyndham (H. S.), *The Annals of Covent Garden Theatre*, 1906, Vol. I.

[1] Wilkinson (Tate), *Memoirs of his Own Life*, 2 Vols., Dublin, 1791. Vol. I., p. 102.

[2] Jackson (John), *History of the Scottish Stage*, 1793, p. 359.

[3] *Harlequin Sorcerer, with the Loves of Pluto and Proserpine*, by Lewis Theobald.

Mᴿ RIDGWAY.

From a print published by W. West, in the British Museum

where Harlequin is hatched from an egg by the rays of the sun.
" From the first chipping of the egg, his receiving motion, his feeling
the ground, his standing upright, to his quick *Harlequin* trip
round the empty shell, through the whole progression, every limb
had its tongue, and every motion a voice, which ' spoke with most
miraculous organ ' to the understandings and sensations of the
observers." [1]   He was famed also for his trick of scratching his
ear like a dog.   Some idea of his agility may be gained from the
account of a certain dance he performed, in which he is said to have
executed three hundred steps in a rapid advance of three yards
only.[2]   He seems to have exercised great care in the selection of
the music to accompany his mimed scenes, for a contemporary
writer declares that " every action was executed to different agree-
able music, so properly adapted that it properly expresses what is
going forward."   Despite his success as Harlequin, he never
conquered his personal belief that he was a great tragic actor, and
declared to a friend that he would rather act tragedy to half-a-dozen
people in the pit than play Harlequin to a crowded house.[3]

In the frontispiece to the third edition of *Harlequin Horace* [4]
(see Pl. fcg. p. 102), Rich, portrayed as Harlequin, stands in an attitude
of triumph, with his bat in one hand and the libretto of the piece
in the other.   The muse of Horace retreats before him, and at his
feet lie the neglected works of Shakespeare, Rowe and Johnson.
If this representation of Rich can be regarded as an authentic
portrait of him in the character, the costume he wore as Harlequin

---

[1] *Op. cit.*, p. 368.

[2] In regard to the particular dancing abilities required of Harlequin, the British
Museum possesses an exceedingly interesting volume entitled *A Chacoon for a
Harlequin. With all the Postures, Attitudes, Motions of the Head and Arms and other
Gestures proper to the Character*, by G. Le Roussau, published at London, 1730.
The general reader will delight in the quaint attitudes, while the studious dancer
will be able to reconstruct the chacoon by means of Feuillet's *Chorégraphie, ou,
L'Art de décrire la Dance*, Paris, 1701 (or the English translation by John Weaver,
Orchesography, 1706), which is the system of notation employed by Le Roussau.
This work seems to us of such importance that we have reproduced it in facsimile
in the Appendix.

[3] Jackson (John), *op. cit.*, p. 363.

[4] *Harlequin Horace, or, The Art of Modern Poetry*, 3rd Edit., 1735.

differed little from that worn by Domenico. The mask is a simplified version of that worn by the Italian actors. The bat is the same short sword, to which, however, Rich seems to have been the first to assign the magic qualities of a conjuror's wand.[1]

Davies declares that :

> Mr. Rich was not only a very artful contriver of that kind of stage entertainment called pantomime, but an admirable actor of Harlequin, the principal character in it. Nor can we boast of any one man who has, during the space of fifty years, approached to his excellences in that part ; his gesticulation was so perfectly expressive of his meaning that every motion of his hand or head, or of any part of his body, was a kind of dumb eloquence that was readily understood by the audience. Mr. Garrick's action was not more perfectly adapted to his characters than Mr. Rich's attitudes and movements to the varied employment of the wooden sword magician. His taking leave of Columbine in one or two of his pantomimes was at once graceful and affecting. His consummate skill in teaching others to express the language of the mind by action, was evident from the great number of actors he produced to fill up the inferior parts of his mimic scenes ; Pantaloon, Pierrot, the Clown, and all the other various characters, he formed himself ; and to his instructions we owe a Hippisley, a Nivelon, a La Guerre, an Arthur, and a Lalause, all excellent performers of these diverting mummeries.[2]

Of his private life, Jackson says " he was an affectionate husband, and a tender father, just in all his dealings, loved conviviality and a friend, and was charitable and humane." [3]   He was very fond of dumb animals, particularly cats. Peg Woffington, who sought an interview with him at his house in Bloomsbury Square, encountered the manager reclining " on a Couch, with one Leg lolling over the other, his left Hand holding a Play-Book, and his right a China Cup, out of which he was sipping some Tea.   Round him, *upon* him, and *about* him, were seven-and-twenty Cats of different Sizes, Ages, and Complexions.   Some were staring him in the Face, some eating the Toast and Butter out of his Mouth,

---

[1] *Cf.* the frontispiece to *Les Fées, ou, Les Contes de Ma Mère l'Oye*, in which Harlequin is shown with one hand resting on his bat, and the other holding a magic wand. (See Gherardi, *Théâtre Italien*, Vol. VI., p. 527.)

[2] *Op. cit.*, Vol. I., pp. 368, 369.

[3] *Op. cit.*, p. 369.

G. Vander Gucht Inv.ᵗ & Sculp.

Shakespear, Rowe, Johnson, now are quite undone
These are thy Tryumphs, thy Exploits O Lun!

THE TRIUMPH OF PANTOMIME

From " Harlequin Horace," 3rd Edit., 1735

MUNDUS TOTUS AGIT HISTRIONEM

The Theatrical Steel-Yards of 1750.

From an engraving in the Burney Collection, in the British Museum

some licking the Cream out of a Cup, some frisking about, some lying down, some perched upon his Knee, some upon his Head."[1]

Rich died on the 26th of November, 1761, at his house in Covent Garden Piazza. He was buried in Hillingdon Churchyard. Soon afterwards Garrick introduced a speaking Harlequin into a revival of his pantomime *Harlequin's Invasion*, and in the prologue to it paid a graceful tribute to the memory of the " father of English Harlequins " :

> But why a speaking Harlequin ? 'Tis wrong,
> The wits will say, to give the fool a tongue.
> When Lun appear'd, with matchless art and whim
> He gave the pow'r of speech to every limb ;
> Tho' mask'd and mute, convey'd his quick intent,
> And told in frolic gestures all he meant ;
> But now the motley coat, and sword of wood,
> Require a tongue to make them understood.

Another eulogium appeared in the *Annual Register* for 1761 :

> ON THE DEATH OF JOHN RICH, ESQ.
> " *Accept this latest tribute at my hand.*"
> The scene is closed. Life's play is done,
> And pleasantry expires with Lun,
> Who well perform'd with various art
> The mimic and the moral part.
> His action just, correct his plan,
> Whether as Harlequin, or man.
> Hear, critics, hear ! and spare your jest,
> Life's but a motley garb at best ;
> He wore it long with grace and ease,
> And ev'ry gesture taught to please.
> Where (some few patchwork foibles seen
> Scattered around—blue—yellow—green)
> His constant virtue's radiant hue
> O'er all superior shone to view,
> The lively vision of repartee
> As magic swords was smart and free,
> Like that, for harmless mirth design'd,
> It struck, but left no pain behind.

[1] *Memoirs of the celebrated Mrs. Woffington*, 1760, p. 20.

The masque of oddity he wore
Endeared the hidden beauties more.
When thrown aside, the shade was clear'd,
The real countenance appear'd,
Where human kindness, candour fair,
And truth, the native features were.
How few like him could change with ease
From shape to shape and all should please !
Think on the num'rous hours of sport
We spent with him in Fancy's Court !
What ev'nings of supreme delight !
They're past, they're clos'd in endless night.
—For gratitude for virtue's cause
Crown his last exit with applause.
Let him not want the lasting praise
(That noble meed of well-spent days),
While this, his mortal dress laid by
With ready grace and decency.
Now changing on a nobler plan
To blissful saint from worthy man,
He makes on yon celestial shore
One easy transformation more.

The next important Harlequin was Henry Woodward, a contemporary of John Rich. The eldest son of a tallow chandler
in Southwark, he was born in London on the 2nd of October, 1714,
and was intended to follow the same trade ; but, owing to his father's
failure in business and being seized with a passion to be an actor,
he joined John Rich's troupe and on the 1st of June, 1729, played
at Lincoln's Inn Fields as the Beggar in a " Lilliputian " version
of *The Beggar's Opera*. Rich, being impressed by the " graceful
deportment and elegant demeanour " of the young actor, trained
him to play Harlequin, which part he first sustained on the 25th of
September, 1734, in *The Cheats, or, The Tavern Bilkers*. He also
played comedy and soon attracted notice for his Setter in *The
Old Batchelor*, and Squire Richard in *The Provoked Husband*. On
the 3rd of January, 1737, under the name of Lun Junior, he played
Harlequin Macheath in a pantomime of his own composition
entitled *The Beggar's Pantomime, or, The Contending Columbines ;*

HENRY WOODWARD

From an old engraving, artist unknown

this piece was inspired by the quarrels between Kitty Clive and Mrs. Cibber as to who should play Polly and who Lucy in *The Beggar's Opera.*

At the end of the season (1737) Woodward went to Drury Lane, where he played until 1741–2. He was much admired as Sir Amorous La Foole, Lord Foppington and Sir Andrew Aguecheek. On the 20th of December, 1741, he appeared as Coachman in *Drummer, or, The Haunted House.* He remained at Drury Lane until 1747, playing the lead in comedy when he was engaged by Sheridan for the Smock Alley Theatre, Dublin, where he first appeared on the 28th of September. On his return to London he again played at Drury Lane.

Between 1751 and 1756, Woodward produced and acted in many pantomimes of his own. One of these, *Queen Mab,* produced in collaboration with Garrick at Drury Lane on the 28th December, 1750, was most successful and ran for forty nights. It was a bitter defeat for Rich, and a print was published, entitled *The Theatrical Steel-yards of* 1750, in which Mrs. Cibber, Mrs. Woffington, Quin and Barry are shown suspended from one arm, which is easily outweighed by Garrick sitting on the other. Near Garrick stands Woodward, holding up Queen Mab in an attitude of triumph, while Rich, crestfallen, lies on the ground.

On the 22nd of October, 1758, Woodward had an offer from Barry to join him as partner in a scheme to build a second theatre in the Crow Street, Dublin. After much cogitation he embarked on the enterprise, which, however, was unsuccessful. He reappeared at Covent Garden on the 5th of October, 1763, his last appearance being on the 13th of January, 1777, when he played Stephano in *The Tempest.* Woodward died on the 17th of April and was buried in the vaults of St. George's, Hanover Square.

As an actor in comedy he had few equals in his day, and " excelled most in parts where nature had stretched her power to ridiculous excess. All the variations of brisk impertinence and assumed consequences, of affected gaiety, unblushing effrontery and lively absurdity, he displayed with a most engaging confidence."[1] He had a tendency to over-act; but his Marplot, Sir Joseph Wittol, Brisk, Boabdil, Tattle and Parolles were considered unequalled. He received the highest terms of any actor of his day.

His graceful figure and the charm of his actions fitted him for the part of Harlequin, which he played with extraordinary success. He was an apt pupil of Rich's, and, like his master, excelled in the difficult art of mime. He was noted for one scene in which he pretended to eat a bunch of currants:

Soft music was played: he came on, sat at a table (on which there was placed *nothing*), and made pretence of taking up the stalk of a bunch of currants. Then, holding high his hand, with the points of finger and thumb compressed, he seemed to shake the stalk, and to strip off the currants with his mouth. In like manner he would appear to hold up a cherry by the stalk, and, after eating it, to spurt the stone from his lips. Eating a gooseberry, paring an apple, sucking an orange or peach—all were simulated in the same marvellous fashion. In short, the audience perfectly knew what fruit he seemed to be eating by the highly ingenious deception of his acting.[2]

He was fond of striking attitudes, and, according to the rhythm of the music, would perform a series of poses in harmony with " the vicissitudes demanded by the various passions represented."

According to the representation of Woodward in the " Steelyard " print described, his costume as Harlequin differed little from that worn by Domenico.

Woodward was well educated, and continually pursued his studies with the aid of a small but select library. He was a silent man, and preferred his own company to that of others, placed his personal interests ever foremost, and when in authority behaved like a bullying tyrant to those under him. He wrote several pantomimes, such as *Harlequin Ranger* (1751), *The Genii* (1752), *Queen Mab* (1752), *Harlequin Fortunatus* (1753), *Proteus, or, Harlequin in China* (1755), and *Mercury Harlequin* (1756). During his last illness he composed a prologue which he never lived to deliver:

[1] Davies, *op. cit.*, Vol. I., p. 302.
[2] Russell (W. Clark), *Representative Actors*, N.D., p. 122.

> Let me not bear too grave a mien,
> But if (a common case) I quit the scene,
> This parting is well made, the farce is o'er,
> And Woodward's voice awakes your mirth no more.

After Woodward, the Harlequin at Covent Garden was Lee Lewes who copied his attitudes. He was succeeded by Boyce.

The great tragedian Edmund Kean played Harlequin with considerable success in his early years. He learned the art of tumbling while travelling with Richardson's Show and Saunders's Circus, and acquired a knowledge of dancing from D'Egville. When he had established his fame in London, he announced that he would appear in pantomime, but, owing to an accident, was forced to abandon his intention at the last moment. Hazlitt, who went full of eagerness to see him, vented his disappointment in these words :

Good reader, it was not the jump through the trap-door that we wished literally to see, but the leap from Othello to Harlequin. What a jump ! What an interval, what a gulf to pass ! What an elasticity of soul and body too—what a diversity of capacity in the same diminutive person ! To be Othello, a man should be all passion, abstraction, imagination : to be Harlequin, he should have his wits in his heels, and in his fingers' ends ! To be both, it is impossible, or miraculous.[1]

When Kean was drawing crowded houses at Drury Lane, the genial Richardson went to see his erstwhile Harlequin play Richard III. After the performance he went to a neighbouring tavern to partake of a " modest half-pint of porter." A bystander inquired of him whether he liked Kean's acting. The showman replied : " Like him, muster ? why he nearly lifted me off my seat in his tent scene. Ah, but that's nothing to his Harlequin. See him hold Columbine on his leg, pitch up a bat and catch it ; that was nature, if you like, and real acting. Good-night, muster." [2]

In 1800, a very successful pantomime was given at Drury Lane

---

[1] Hazlitt (William), *Criticisms and Dramatic Essays of the English Stage*, 1851, pp. 253, 254.
[2] Stirling (Edward), *Old Drury Lane*, 2 Vols., 1881, Vol. I., p. 41.

entitled *Harlequin Amulet, or, The Magic of Mona.* This was distinguished by several new features in Harlequin's costume. James Byrne, who played this character, appeared in " a white silk-shape, fitting without a wrinkle, and into which the variegated silk patches were woven, the whole profusely covered with spangles, and presenting a very sparkling appearance." [1]

Byrne, who had been a member of the ballet at Drury Lane in Garrick's time, also introduced several changes in the " business " associated with this character. Previously it had been a feature of the English interpretation that the actor should conclude each phase of mime with one of the five fixed poses of Harlequin, which represented respectively Admiration, Defiance, Determination, Flirtation, and Thought. He abolished this tradition, and invented a diversity of new " attitudes." He also gave a reason for the colours comprised in the costume. Red symbolised temper ; blue, love ; yellow, jealousy ; brown or mauve, constancy. When Harlequin wore his mask down he was supposed to be invisible, and when his wand was filched from his grasp he was supposed to fall into the power of the Clown. [2]

According to Grimaldi, " Mr. James Byrne was at that time the best Harlequin on the boards, and never has been excelled, even if equalled, since that period." [3]

Byrne [4] was at Covent Garden in 1805, but in the following year was succeeded by John Bologna. The latter played Harlequin at the Royal Circus from 1795 to 1802, when he became attached to Sadler's Wells, where for many years he played Harlequin to Grimaldi's Clown. Kemble, watching him play Oscar in *Oscar*

---

[1] *Memoirs of Joseph Grimaldi.* Edit. by Boz, New Edit., 1903, p. 78.

[2] *Cf.* Grimaldi, *op. cit.*, p. 185 (footnote), for James Smith's poem on Grimaldi :

" When Harlequin, his charmer to regain,
Courts her embrace in many a queer disguise,
The light of heels looks for his sword in vain—
Thy furtive fingers snatch the magic prize."

[3] *Op. cit.*, p. 78.

[4] Very little is known of this Harlequin. He died on the 4th of December, 1845, at the advanced age of eighty-nine.

A REGENCY HARLEQUIN (1810)

From a collection relating to Sadler's Wells, in the British Museum

and Malvina, remarked : " If that man could speak as well as he acts pantomime, I would never appear again on the stage." There is a reference to him in *Joseph's Lament :*

> Never shall old Bologna—old, alack !
> Once he was young and diamonded all o'er—
> Take his particular Joseph on his back
> And dance the matchless fling, so loved of yore.

Bologna died in poverty at Glasgow, at the age of seventy-one.

Like so many Harlequins, he was more than once a victim of carelessness or spite on the part of the stage hands. On one occasion, as he jumped through a clock-case, there being no one to catch him, he fell and broke his collar bone. As these leaps were an integral part of Harlequin's performance, he had another Harlequin, Tom Ellar, to double him at such moments.

During the Regency other changes were made in Harlequin's dress. He wore a black, two-cornered hat ; the colours were disposed in narrow, isosceles triangles, and his belt was of black velvet instead of leather. The neck opening was V-shaped, and a strip of black velvet ran down the spine and continued upwards to meet the base of the " V " ; sometimes a thin strip of the same material outlined the seams of the tights. The feet were covered with black, unblocked ballet-shoes. The mask was a black vizard, the sword a long and slender lath.

Tom Ellar was born in 1780, and made his first bow in town at the Royalty Theatre on Easter Monday in 1808.[1] In 1809 he took part in a pantomime entitled *The Mountain Witches, or, Harlequin Miller,* produced at the Crow Street Theatre, Dublin. Four years later he began his career at Covent Garden in *Harlequin and the Swans,*[2] and on the 11th of April, 1814, made the first of many appearances at Sadler's Wells in *The Rival Genii, or, Harlequin Wild Man.*

Ellar was so celebrated for his leaps and vaults that any parti-

---

[1] Grimaldi, *op. cit.,* p. 97 (footnote).
[2] Produced December 27th, 1813.

cularly difficult feat of agility came to be termed *à la Ellar*. He, too, was a victim [1] of negligence or malice, for during the run at Covent Garden of the pantomime *Baron Munchausen, or, The Fountain of Love*,[2] after jumping through the " moon " he was allowed to fall and, putting out his hand to save himself, broke his wrist. Ellar was famed for his dangerous feats. On one occasion he " flew from the back of the gallery to the extremity of the stage." He almost invariably concluded a series of " attitudes " with a dazzling pirouette.

Leigh Hunt has left us a picture in prose of the sprightly Harlequin :

> In comes Harlequin, demi-masked, party-coloured, nimble-toed, lithe, agile ; bending himself now this way, now that ; bridling up like a pigeon ; tipping out his toe like a dancer ; then taking a fantastic skip ; then standing ready at all points, and at right angles with his omnipotent lath-sword, the emblem of the converting power of fancy and light-heartedness. Giddy as we think him, he is resolved to show us that his head can bear more giddiness than we fancy ; and lo ! beginning with it by degrees, he whirls it round into a very spin, with no more remorse than if it were a button. Then he draws his sword, slaps his enemy, who has just come upon him, into a settee ; and springing upon him, dashes through the window like a swallow.[3]

Poor Ellar ! As age and illness racked his frame, he gradually declined in popularity, passed from the theatres to sordid East End music-halls, and at last to the streets. Thackeray has drawn a sad picture of the old Harlequin in his decline :

> Our Harlequin Ellar, prince of many of our enchanted islands, was he not at Bow Street the other day, in his dirty, faded, tattered motley seized as a law-breaker for acting at a penny theatre, after having well nigh starved in the streets, where nobody would listen to his guitar ? No one gave him a shilling to bless him, not one of us who owe him so much.

In 1840, a benefit was given for him at the Victoria, and two years later he shed his motley for ever.

[1] See Lewes (C. L.), *Memoirs of Lee Lewes*, 4 Vols., 1805. Vol. I., p. 67, for an account of an accident that happened to the Harlequin Lee Lewes.
[2] Produced December 26th, 1816.
[3] *Essays*, 1887, p. 100.

TOM ELLAR AS HARLEQUIN

From a water-colour drawing by H. Brown, in the British Museum

About this period black was introduced into the patches of the costume and the colours received a new significance; red symbolised fire; blue, water; yellow, air; and black, earth.

One of the last of English Harlequins was Fred Leoville, of the Britannia, who died in 1922.

List of Principal Works Consulted

ANDREINI (ISABELLA). *Fragmenti di alcune scritture . . . raccolti da F. Andreini, e dati in luce da F. Scala.* Venetia. 1647.
Le Rime d'Isabella Andreini. Napoli. 1696.

ANON. *British Stage, The ; or, The Exploits of Harlequin :* a Farce, designed as an After Entertainment for the Audiences of Harlequin Doctor Faustus and the Necromancer. London. 1724.

ANON. *Glimpses of Real Life as seen in the Theatrical World and in Bohemia :* Being the Confessions of Peter Paterson, a Strolling Comedian. Edinburgh. 1864.

BASCHET (ARMAND). *Les comédiens italiens à la cour de France sous Charles IX., Henri III., Henri IV., et Louis XIII.* Paris. 1882.

CAMPARDON (EMILE). *Les Comédiens du Roi de la Troupe Italienne.* Paris. 2 Vols. 1880.

CAPRIN (GIULIO). *Carlo Goldoni : la sua vita—le sue opere.* Milano. 1907.

CHATFIELD-TAYLOR (H. C.). *Goldoni, A Biography.* London. 1914.

CHURCHILL (CHARLES). *The Rosciad.* 9th ed. London. 1765.

CIBBER (COLLEY). *An Apology for the Life of Mr. Colley Cibber.* 4th ed. London. 1740.

DASENT (J. R.). Ed. *Acts of the Privy Council of England,* 1552–1591. London. 20 Vols. 1890–1900.

DAVIES (THOMAS). *Memoirs of the Life of David Garrick.* New ed. London. 2 Vols. 1808.

DIBDIN (THOMAS). *Harlequin Hoax ; or, A Pantomime Proposed :* A Comic Extravaganza. London. 1814.

DISHER (M. WILLSON). *Clowns and Pantomimes.* London. 1925.

DUCHARTRE (P. L.). *La Comédie Italienne.* Nouv. édit. Paris. 1925.

ESTOILE (PIERRE DE L'). *Mémoirs-Journaux.* Paris. 12 Vols. 1875.

FEUILLERAT (ALBERT). Ed. *Documents relating to the Office of the Revels in the time of Queen Elizabeth.* London. 1908. (*Materialen zur Kunde des älteren englischen Dramas.* Vol. 21.)

GHERARDI (EVARISTO). *Le Théâtre Italien de Gherardi, ou le Recueil Général de toutes les comédies et scènes Françaises jouées par les Comédiens Italiens du Roi pendant tout le temps qu'ils ont été au service.* Paris. 6 Vols. Eds. of 1717 and 1741.

GOLDONI (CARLO). *Memoirs of.* Translated from the original French by John Black. London. 2 Vols. 1814.

GOZZI (COUNT CARLO). *Memoirs of.* Translated into English by J. A. Symonds. With Essays on Italian Impromptu Comedy, Gozzi's Life, the Dramatic Fables and Pietro Longhi, by the Translator. London. 2 Vols. 1890.

GREG (W. W.). Ed. *Henslowe's Diary*, 1591–1609. London. 1904–08. Ed. *Henslowe Papers*, being documents supplementary to *Henslowe's Diary.* London. 1907.

GRIMALDI (JOSEPH). *Memoirs of Joseph Grimaldi.* Ed. by Boz. New Ed. 1903.

GRIMM ET DIDEROT. *Correspondance Littéraire, Philosophique et Critique adressée à un Souverain d'Allemagne.* Paris. 17 Vols. 1812–14.

HAZLITT (WILLIAM). *Criticisms and Dramatic Essays of the English Stage.* London. 1851.

HEYWOOD (THOMAS). *Apology for Actors*, in three books. (From ed. of 1612.) London. 1841. (Shakespeare Society Publications.)

HUNT (LEIGH). *Essays.* London. 1887.

JACKSON (JOHN). *History of the Scottish Stage.* London. 1793.

JAL (AUGUSTE). *Dictionnaire critique de Biographie et d'Histoire, errata et supplément pour tous les dictionnaires historiques d'après des documents authentiques inédits.* Paris. 1867.

LAMBRANZI (GREGORIO). *Neue und Curieuse Theatralische Tantz-Schule.* Nuremberg. 1716.

LE ROUSSAU (G.). *A Chacoon for a Harlequin.* With all the Postures, Attitudes, Motions of the Head and Arms and other Gestures proper to the Character. London. 1730.

LEWES (C. L.). *Memoirs of Lee Lewes.* London. 4 Vols. 1805.

MANTZIUS (KARL). *A History of Theatrical Art in Ancient and Modern Times.* Translated by Louise von Cossel. London. 6 Vols. 1903–21.

MARTINELLI (TRISTANO). *Compositions de Rhétorique de M. Don Arlequin.* Paris. *c.* 1601 (?).

MOLAND (LOUIS). *Molière et la comédie italienne.* Paris. 1867.

LIST OF PRINCIPAL WORKS CONSULTED

NASHE (THOMAS). *Works.* Ed. by R. B. McKerrow. London. 5 Vols. 1904–10.

NICHOLS (J.). *Progresses and Public Processions of Queen Elizabeth.* London. 3 Vols. New Ed. 1823.

PLANCHÉ (J. R.). *Recollections and Reflections.* Rev. Ed. London. 1901.

RASI (LUIGI). *I Comici Italiani : biografia, bibliografia, iconografia.* Firenze. 2 Vols. 1894–1905.

RICCOBONI (LUIGI). *Histoire de l'ancien théâtre Italien depuis la décadence de la comédie latine, avec un catalogue des tragédies et comédies italiennes imprimées depuis l'an 1500 jusqu'à l'an 1650.* Paris. 1728.

RUSSELL (W. CLARK). *Representative Actors.* London. N.D.

SAND (MAURICE). *Masques et Buffons.* Paris. 2 Vols. 1860.

SCHERILLO (DR. MICHELE). *La Commedia dell' Arte in Italia.* Torino. 1884.

SMITH (DR. WINIFRED). *The Commedia dell' Arte.* New York. 1912.

STIRLING (EDWARD). *Old Drury Lane.* London. 2 Vols. 1881.

VAUQUELIN (SIEUR DE LA FRESNAYE). *Diverses Poésies.* Caen. 1612.

WALPOLE (HORACE). *The Letters of Horace Walpole, Earl of Oxford.* Ed. by P. Cunningham. London. 9 Vols. 1858.

WEAVER (JOHN). *The History of Mimes and Pantomimes.* London. 1728.

WILKINSON (TATE). *Memoirs of his Own Life.* Dublin. 2 Vols. 1791.

WOFFINGTON (PEG). *Memoirs of the celebrated Mrs. Woffington.* London. 1760.

Calendar of State Papers. Foreign Series of the Reign of Elizabeth. 1569–71.

Mercure de France. 1741.

A Chacoon for a Harlequin

With all the Postures, Attitudes,
motions of the Head and Arms,
and other Gestures proper
to this Character.

Being the first that ever appear'd in this Gust

Compos'd Writt in
Characters and
Engraved by

F: Le Roussau Dancing-master

LONDON
and sold by y author in St albans-Street and att mr Barretts
musik-shop at the Harp & Crown in Pickadily.

to Mr Louis Dupré

Sir

The neatnefs with wich you perform ÿ Character of
Harlequin in all ÿ different Attitudes wich belong to it
they wich you give with so much Grace & supplenefs;
obliges me to take ÿ liberty to offer you this little work. it
being ÿ first of this kind that ever yet appeard in
publick. My chief design being to discribe on
paper. ÿ postures wᶜʰ are most in practice for the
Harlequin, I have endeavour'd to represent some of
yours. but however without pretending (by these
figures) to demonstrate ÿ Excellency of your motions,
ÿ Exactenefs & subtility of wᶜʰ Sir prizes so agreably;
it is a Task I leave to more expert Drawers than
I can pretend to be; whom neverthelefs woud think my
self sufficiently recompensed of my Pains if with
your approbation (wich will draw ÿ regard of those
of our profeffion) I have also ÿ satisfaction to see them exited
thereby, to render more perfect this sort of Choregraphie, or
discription of Dances & attitudes. I am with all ÿ Consideration
& Esteem imaginable.

Sir

your most humble
& most obedient Servant
F: Le Roufsau

To the Reader

Severall persons having desired I woud present ÿ Publick with those Harlequinades I had made but for my own use.

I have endeavour'd to make them as Perfect and as usefull as possible, and I doubt not but those who will excamine them with Care will find them satisfactory.

You shall see in each page the attitude or full posture the Harlequin must be in when he begins each part, and as no person ever attempted to writ the Harlequinades before. I think it necefsary to explain the different Motions of ÿ Head, and the postures in this Chacoon.

Though the motions of ÿ Arms are fully discribed in ÿ first Collection of Mr Feuillet, I have observ'd that few Dancers minded them though they are very necefsary for this sort of Character and for that reason I explain the turnings & motions of the Arm's for this Dance only. and I shall do ÿ same in all ÿ other Dance's I shall here after give to ÿ publick.

N:B: I could not observe ÿ same rules for ÿ motions of ÿ Head as Mr Feuillet has given in his first book. because ÿ situation of ÿ picture Could not allow it. you must only observe that it matters not whether the picture is on ÿ right or left side of ÿ line look only on ÿ true situation of ÿ picture.

Explanation

Face strait forwards...............................

Face turn'd to ỹ left. or. looking over ỹ left shoulder.

face turn'd to ỹ right. or. looking over ỹ right shoulder.

Leaning ỹ head down on ỹ left shoulder

Leaning ỹ head down on ỹ right shoulder.

Stretching ỹ nek and head forwards without moving ỹ shoulders...............................

The Hatt...

Motions of ỹ Arms

it is to be observ'd that there is no alterations in ỹ rules of M.ʳ ferullel excepting I add to ỹ arm a little half moon to represent ỹ hand wich takes off. or putts on ỹ hatt.

Example

To Raise your right arm as high as your Head ⋯⋯⋯⋯

to lower it in a line with $\check{y}$ shoulder, ⋯⋯⋯⋯⋯⋯

to Stretch y^e arm forwards draw it back again then
move it forwards again, w^h is $\check{y}$ Salutation of an Harlequin

to raise $\check{y}$ arm turning $\check{y}$ wrist to put on $\check{y}$ hatt ⋯⋯⋯⋯

to turn your arm round your Shoulder ⋯⋯⋯⋯⋯

you shall know by a stroke of $\check{y}$ pen in what time and
with what steps you must make your motions of $\check{y}$ head, or
turnings of $\check{y}$ arms .

Example

to Carry your right hand to your hatt ⋯⋯⋯

to pull off your hatt

to putt on $\check{y}$ hatt again turning your wrist

125

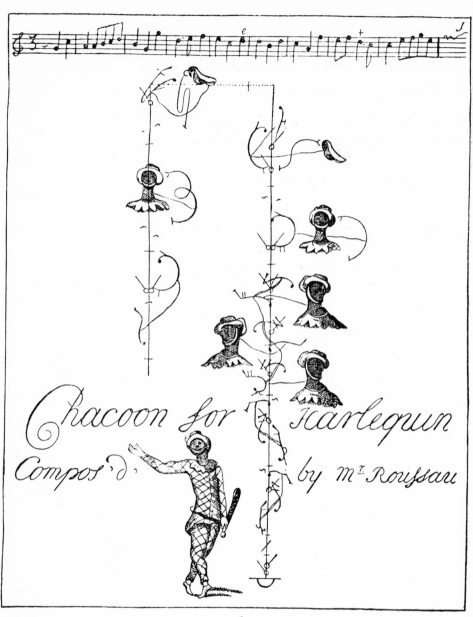

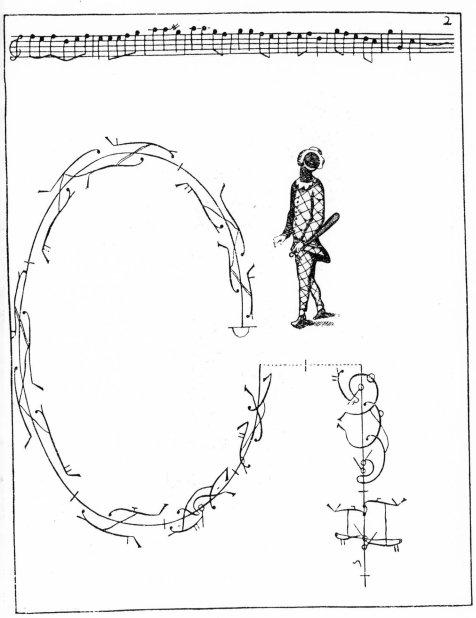

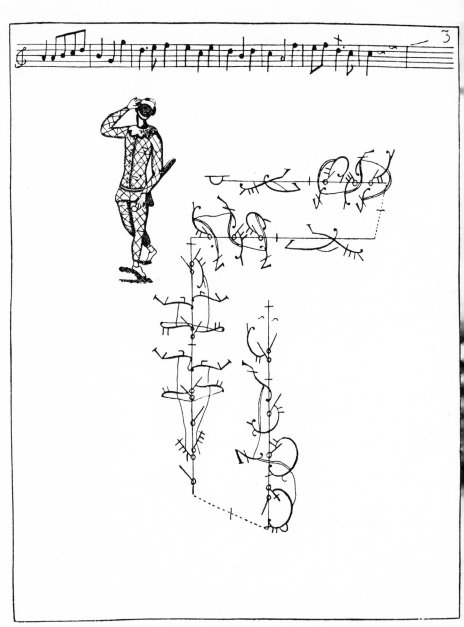

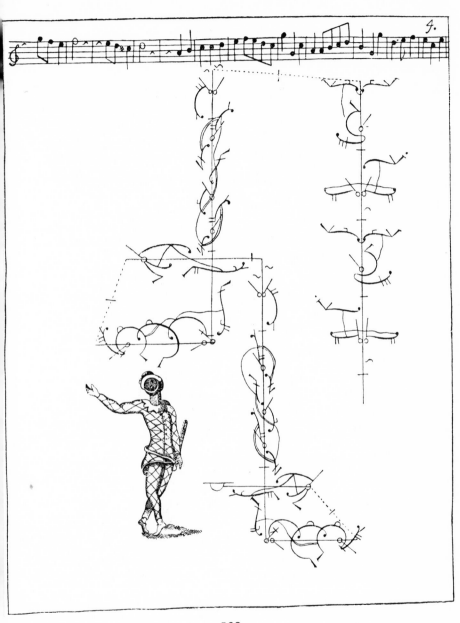

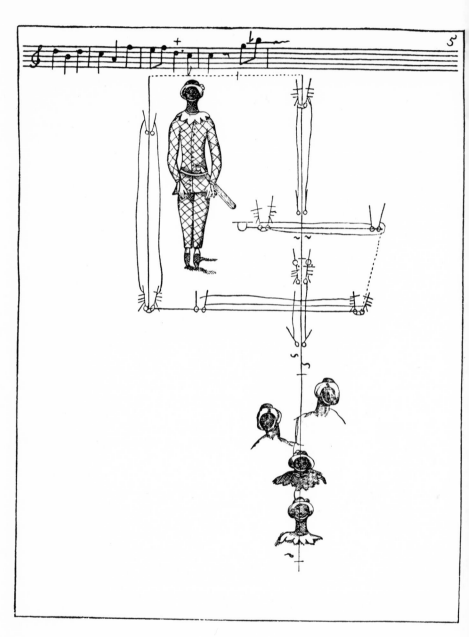

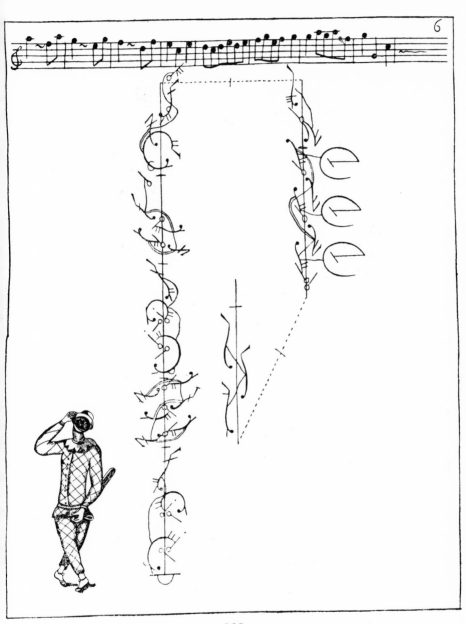

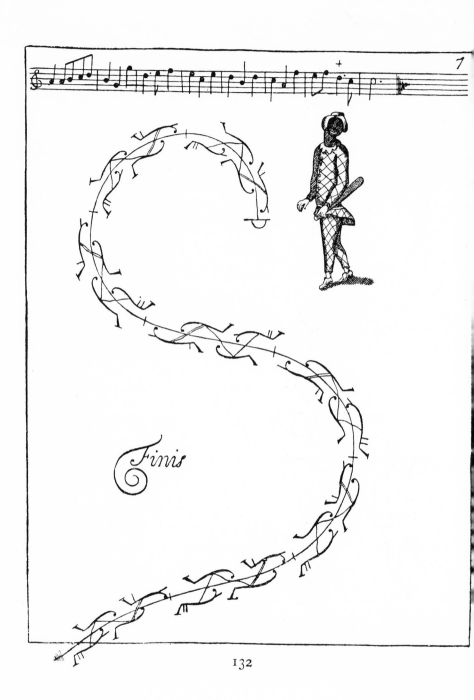

Finis

Harlequin & Mother Goose; or, The Golden Egg.

A Comic Pantomime by Thomas Dibdin

Harlequin & Mother Goose; or, The Golden Egg.

A Comic Pantomime by Thomas Dibdin

The Overture and Music composed by Mr. Ware. The Pantomime produced under the direction of Mr. Farley. The Dances by Mr. Bologna, Jun. The Scenery by Messrs. Phillips, Whitmore, Hollogan, Grieve, Hodgings, and their Assistants.

CAST

as first performed at the Theatre Royal, Covent Garden, on Monday, December 29th, 1806.

MOTHER GOOSE	MR. SIMMONS.
COLIN (*afterwards Harlequin*) . .	MR. KING and MR. BOLOGNA, Jun.
AVARO (*afterwards Pantaloon*) . .	MR. L. BOLOGNA.
'SQUIRE BUGLE (*afterwards Clown*).	MR. GRIMALDI.
BEADLE	MR. DENMAN.
LANDLORD	MR. BOLOGNA.
WOODCUTTER	MR. TRUMAN.
CABIN BOY (*with a song*) . . .	MR. SMALLEY.
SERGEANT	MR. BANKS.

Gardeners : Messrs. DAVIS, DICK, and MORELLI.

Waiters : Messrs. BAKER and GRIFFITHS.

ODDFISH . . . . . MR. MENAGE.

Villagers, etc.: Messrs. ABBOT, T. BLANCHARD, BROWN, BURDEN, EVERARD, FAIRBROTHER, FAIRCLOUGH, GOODWIN, LEE, LINTON, MEYERS, MONK, W. MURRAY, ODWELL, PLATT, POWERS, REEVES, RIMSDYCK, SARJANT, STREET, TETT, J. TETT, THOMAS and WILDE.

Fairies : Masters BENSON, GOODWIN, MORELLI, and SEARLE.

COLUMBINE : Miss SEARLE.   WOODCUTTER'S WIFE : Mrs. WHITMORE.

Villagers, Fairies, etc.: Mesdames BENSON, BOLOGNA, BRISTOW, COX, CRANFIELD, FINDLAY, FOLLET, GRIMALDI, ILIFF, LESERVE, MASTERS, PRICE, SLADER, WATTS.

133

Scene Painters' Plot

Scene 1.—A Village with storm ; Church with churchyard ; bridge, water, moving objects.   Rainbow Cottage and Mansion, R.   Tombstone with inscription, " In Memory of Xantippe, Wife of Bullface Bugle, Esquire " ; Mother Goose on a gander.

Scene 2.—Thick Wood on one side ; entrance on the other ; thick foliage, and an owl seated on a branch, L.   Changes to Mother Goose's cottage.

Scene 3.—A Hall ; a clock with two faces to it, one with a sportsman with his gun.

Scene 4.—A Sea, etc.

Scene 5.—An old Country Inn, with trick sign-post ; rum puncheon to change to a barrow.

Scene 6.—The Inside of Inn, with trick tables and chairs ; Club Rules for Harlequin to jump through.

Scene 7.—A View in a Market Town.

Scene 8.—A Woodcutter's Cottage ; drop wood, etc. ; trick wheel to Fortune, etc.

Scene 9.—A Pavilion by Moonlight ; two trick banks to a steel trap and spring gun.

Scene 10.—A Flower Garden, with three trick tubs, two of them to the statues of Harlequin and Columbine, the other to trick sunflower.

Scene 11.—A View of Golden Square, with trick balcony.

Scene 12.—St. Dunstan's Church, with trick figures and dial.

Scene 13.—An entrance to Vauxhall Gardens.

Scene 14.—Orchestra in Vauxhall Gardens, illuminated as on a gala night.

Scene 15.—Grocer's Shop and Post Office, with trick letter-box to a lion's head ; two trick tea-chests to a sideboard ; and a beehive.

Scene 16.—Grocer's Parlour, with trick sideboard.

Scene 17.—Interior of a Farmyard ; trick beehive.

Scene 18.—Mermaid's Cave, with Sea.

Scene 19.—A Submarine Palace.

Carpenters' Scene Plot

Scene 1.—Set Village, with storm; water bridge; with Church and churchyard, tombstones. Cottage and Mansion, R.; with moving objects across the bridge, etc.; mail coach, waggon, small boats.

Scene 2.—A Wood, to change to Cottage, etc.

Scene 3.—A Hall; panel to turn round; trick clock jump for Harlequin, the clock door to open; little Harlequin is discovered. Trick clock face.

Scene 4.—A Sea.

Scene 5.—A Country Inn, with trick sign-post to a barrow; garden chair, etc.

Scene 6.—Inside of Inn, with trick table, etc.; chairs; and jump for Harlequin.

Scene 7.—A View in a Market Town.

Scene 8.—Woodcutter's Cottage, R.; wood to drop, with trick wheel to Fortune, etc.

Scene 9.—A Pavilion Moonlight; two trick banks.

Scene 10.—A Flower Garden, with three trick tubs.

Scene 11.—Golden Square, with trick balcony.

Scene 12.—St. Dunstan's Church, with trick figures and dial.

Scene 13.—Entrance to Vauxhall Gardens.

Scene 14.—Orchestra in Vauxhall Gardens.

Scene 15.—Grocer's Shop and Post Office, with trick letter-box, and two trick tea-chests, etc.

Scene 16.—Grocer's Parlour, with trick sideboard.

Scene 17.—A Farmyard, with trick beehives, etc.

Scene 18.—Mermaid's Cave with Sea.

Scene 19.—A Submarine Palace.

Property Plot

Scene 1.—Thunder, etc. ; stick for Mother Goose ; favours for Villagers ; Huntsman's whip ; staff for Beadle.

Scene 2.—Golden Egg ; goose.

Scene 3.—Three chairs ; a knife and stick for Pantaloon ; a sword for Harlequin ; two pistols to fire behind the scenes.

Scene 4.—

Scene 5.—Two jugs (one with bran in it, the other with beer) ; drum and fife ; some apples ; two purses for Pantaloon, etc.

Scene 6.—-Cloths and newspaper for Waiters ; pie with a live duck in it ; two knives and two forks ; two chairs ; saw ; snuff-box, etc.

Scene 7.—Masks and heads for Morris Dancers, etc.

Scene 8.—Bundle of wood for Woodcutter ; some money.

Scene 9.—Gun to fire behind the scenes.

Scene 10.—Two sunflowers to open.

Scene 11.—

Scene 12.—Pieman's basket ; a Jew's bag with jacket and two hats in it, which changes to two bells.

Scene 13.—Cocked hat and a large sword ; bread and ham.

Scene 14.—Tables set out for supper ; fowls, fish, and plates to fly up ; several masks, tin fish-kettle, broom, ladle, and whisk for Clown.

Scene 15.—Some letters, one with a note in it ; bell for Postman, Baker, basket, loaves, etc. ; Blackamoor's head, etc.

Scene 16.—Two chairs ; trick bottle, with fireworks in it.

Scene 17.—Two beehives and bees.

Scene 18.—Two shells ; seaweed ; and golden egg.

Scene 19.—Wands.

Mother Goose; or, The Golden Egg

SCENE FIRST.—*A Village, with storm, etc. ; Sunset ; on the R. are the entrance gates to Squire Bugle's Mansion, adjoining to it Colin's Cottage. A Church with the churchyard in front, L. ; the perspective a distant view of a river and a bridge over it* (1) [1]; *moving objects both on the river and bridge* (2). *During the storm* MOTHER GOOSE *has raised, she is seen descending from the skies mounted on a gander ; after the storm* (3) *the clouds disperse, and a Rainbow is seen, the Sun rises gradually, etc., etc. ; its golden beams are finely reflected on the window of the Church. A crowd of Male and Female Peasants assemble, decorated with favours, to celebrate the nuptials of the* SQUIRE *and* COLINETTE ; *some dance while others sing the following :*

CHORUS

Neighbours, we're met on a very merry morning,
   Lads and lasses dressed in all their pride so gay,
To celebrate the happy hour, when maiden shyness scorning,
   Sweet COLINETTE is married to the SQUIRE to-day.
        Old and young
        Join in the throng,
     Cutting nimble capers,
       Haste to the church,
       In the lurch
    Leaving care and vapours.
      No one sad,
      Hey ! go mad.
Man and maiden seem to say,
       If I knew who
      Prove but true,
The next may be my wedding day.

Enter AVARO, *L., leading* COLINETTE (6). *Bugle solo* (7). *Enter the* SQUIRE *from the mansion, equipped for hunting, preceded by* HUNTSMEN, JOCKEYS, GROOMS, *and* SERVANTS. AVARO *presents* COLINETTE *to the* SQUIRE ; *she turns from him and welcomes* COLIN, *who appears at the window of cottage ; the* GUARDIAN *interferes ;* COLINETTE *approaches and points to the tomb* (9) *of the Squire's late wife, which is seen in the centre of the churchyard, bearing the following inscription :*

---

[1] The figures denote the changes in the music.

In Memory

OF

XANTIPPE

WIFE OF

BULLFACE BUGLE, ESQ.,

when the SQUIRE *jocularly sings the old air of* (10)

First wife's dead,
There let her lie ;
She's at rest,
And so am I.

(11) *etc., etc.* (12) *the* SQUIRE, AVARO, *and* COLINETTE *with* HUNTSMEN, *etc., march in procession, but are interrupted by* COLIN, *who enters from his cottage ;* COLINETTE, *from an impulse of love,* (13) *flies to him for protection ; they are separated by* AVARO, *who with the* SQUIRE, COLINETTE, *etc., sings the following:*

(14) *Sestetto and Chorus.*

COLIN. When guardians break a promise due,
SQUIRE. Who dare our progress stop ?
AVARO. When richer suitors come to woo,
SQUIRE. Such folks as you may hop.
COLINETTE. Yet listen to the injured youth.
AVARO. Your dignity he mocks (*to* SQUIRE).
COLIN. I claim her hand.
SQUIRE. Indeed, forsooth ! I'll put him in the stocks.
   Then merrily, merrily march away,
   For this shall be my wedding day.
CHORUS (15). Then merrily, merrily march away,
   It is the Squire's wedding day.
COLIN.   This should have been my wedding day.

A BEADLE *and* COUNTRYMAN *enter L., with* MOTHER GOOSE *in custody as a reputed witch ; the* BEADLE *addresses the* SQUIRE *as follows :*

BEADLE (16). So please, your worship, ere we go,
   Punish this wicked witch.
MOTHER G.   O fie !
   Good neighbours, why d'ye use me so ?
   Indeed, no wicked witch am I.
COLIN. Pity her age.
MOTHER G. Pray let me loose,
   Don't hurt poor harmless Mother Goose.
BEADLE (*to* COLIN). Out of the way, officious fool ;
SQUIRE. Go—take her to the ducking stool.

138

COLIN. Shame, neighbours, shame !
SQUIRE. Don't list to him ;
But try if she chance to sink or swim.
Meantime merrily march away,
Because this is my wedding day.
CHORUS (17). Merrily, merrily, march away,
And keep the Squire's wedding day.

While they sing the chorus COLIN *rescues* MOTHER GOOSE *from the* BEADLE
and COUNTRYMEN, *who makes her exit—she is seen to ascend as before.* (18)
The SQUIRE (19) *approaches his late wife's tomb and strikes it with his whip.*
The tomb opens and her ghost appears (20), *which* MOTHER GOOSE *has raised,*
clad in white satin and poppy ribbons, follows the SQUIRE, *shakes her hands at*
him, and descends through a trap. The SQUIRE *runs off terrified, R.* (21)
Meantime COLIN *and* COLINETTE *are conversing with one another—they both*
exit, L.

SCENE SECOND.—*Mother Goose's Retreat. The front a thick wood, on one*
side an entrance, on the other thick foliage, etc. ; an Owl seated on a branch, very
prominent in the perspective ; a clear blue sky with moon and stars, etc.

MOTHER GOOSE *enters, and sings the following :*

(22) *Air and Chorus.*

The grasshopper chirrups—listen, listen,
The cricket chimes in with the sound ;
On water and windows the moonbeams glisten,
And dewdrops bespangle the ground.

Then haste from dog-rose, briar and bell,
From dingle, brake, or daisied dell,
Collect each potent fairy spell
Our magic can produce

To plague yon Squire, and to aid
Young Colin to obtain the maid ;
And when my orders are obeyed
You'll laugh with Mother Goose.

CHORUS (*from without*). Ha, ha, ha !—ha, ha, ha !
We'll laugh with Mother Goose.
MOTHER G. Now softly see Aurora's blush
Bids cease your revels—hush, hush, hush !
CHORUS. Hush, hush, hush !
(23) MOTHER GOOSE *waves her stick, when four* SPRITES *enter, they dance*
round her, and afterwards retire—the wood on the R. side opens and presents
Mother Goose's Habitation.

139

MOTHER GOOSE *exits into her cottage.* (24) COLIN *enters in a very despond-ing state.* MOTHER GOOSE *suddenly approaches to address him in these lines with action appropriate :*

MOTHER GOOSE.   Youth, why despair ?   The girl thou shalt obtain ;
     This present shall her guardian's sanction gain.

    (25) *The* GOOSE *appears.*

    Nay, doubt not, while she's kindly used, she'll lay
    A golden egg on each succeeding day ;
    You served me—no reply—there lies your way.

(26) MOTHER GOOSE *exits.* COLIN *appears struck with surprise, feeds and makes much of the* GOOSE, *and on looking up his wonder is increased by the disappearance of her cottage. The scene during this period changes to her retreat as before.* COLIN *and* GOOSE *exit, L.*

SCENE THIRD.—*A Hall in Avaro's House.*

(27) COLINETTE *enters, followed by* AVARO, *and soon after,* COLIN, *L.* AVARO *endeavours to turn him out, when* COLIN *shows him the golden egg.* (28) COLIN *brings in the* GOOSE *and explains what wealth he may possess. Avarice gets the better of* AVARO'S *promise to the* SQUIRE. COLIN *presents him with the golden egg, and he joins* COLIN *and* COLINETTE'S *hands, but presuming he shall gain all the gold at once by destroying the* GOOSE, *he draws his knife, and is preparing to murder it,* (29) *which* COLIN *prevents.* (30) SQUIRE *enters.* COLIN, *fearful of losing his prize, consents rashly to the sacrifice of the bird. The* GOOSE *now makes her exit through a panel in the back scene, which turns round and presents* MOTHER GOOSE, (31) *who seizes the egg, addresses* AVARO *as follows :*

MOTHER GOOSE.   Thou avaricious, selfish, ingrate elf,
     Like other fools too cunning for thyself !
     Thy ward shall still perplex you by her flight—
     Lo ! thus I change the lovers (32).

(COLINETTE *is changed to* COLUMBINE *and* COLIN *to* HARLEQUIN.)

            Motley white,
    Thou too shalt wander till this egg of gold,
    Which in the sea I cast, you once again behold.
       The scene opens and discovers (33)

SCENE FOURTH.—*The Sea.*

MOTHER GOOSE *throws the golden egg into the sea. Scene changes back to Avaro's Hall.*

MOTHER G. Stop, fool! Some recompense is yet thy due. (*To the* SQUIRE) Take that. (*Changes him to* CLOWN.) (34) While thou (*to* AVARO) shalt wear my livery too. (*Changes him to* PANTALOON) (35).

AIR.—Mother Goose.

For slighted kindness take your due ;
  Yet mirth shall with your toils entwine ;
Be Harlequin—while you pursue,
  Not Colinette, but Columbine.
This gift receive (*gives* HARLEQUIN *the sword*), amend what's past,
And guard it better than the last ;
Regain the egg, and happy be,
Till then, farewell !—remember me !

(37) MOTHER GOOSE *retires, and the comic business begins here. They endeavour to secure* HARLEQUIN, *who eludes their grasp, and leaps through the face of the clock, which immediately presents a* SPORTSMAN *with his gun cocked. The* CLOWN *opens the clock door, and a little Harlequin appears as a pendulum, the* CLOWN *saying* " Present ! fire ! " *the* SPORTSMAN *lets off his piece,* (38) *the* CLOWN *falls down, during which period* COLUMBINE *and* HARLEQUIN, *who had previously entered through the panel, escape. After some tricks, the* CLOWN *runs off in pursuit with* PANTALOON *on his back.*

SCENE FIFTH.—*A country inn* (39) *in the front of which is a sign-post,* " Chequers," *and on it a large puncheon, with the word* " Rum " ; *a garden seat is on one side of the door, etc.*

Enter a Recruiting Party. They beat up for Recruits, and various characters enter, amongst which is the CLOWN, *who runs off terrified at the drum. A drunken Cobbler is the only recruit gained, who with the Recruiting Party enters the inn.* (40) HARLEQUIN *and* COLUMBINE *enter, L., and go into the Inn ; and soon after* HARLEQUIN *is seen at the window of it.* PANTALOON *and* CLOWN *enter, L., place themselves on each end of the garden seat ;* HARLEQUIN *waves his sword. They are thrown against each other off the seat. They change situations, and the like again takes place.* (41) *The* CLOWN *knocks smartly at the door ; the* LANDLORD *appears with a full jug ; the* CLOWN *strikes him on the belly as he comes out, upon which he throws the contents of the jug in his face ; a fracas ensues ; they perceive* HARLEQUIN *at the window, and they exit into the house.* HARLEQUIN *leaps from the window, smacks his sword, and the rum puncheon descends from the sign-post, which he transforms into a fruit barrow,* (42) *and a painted puncheon, with a Bacchus astride, ascends in its place ; the* LANDLORD *comes out of his house, and is struck with the change, but wishing for his puncheon again,* HARLEQUIN *changes the painted one into a rum puncheon as before ; the* LANDLORD *exits ; he now throws off his Harlequin's dress, and*

141

appears a complete St. Giles's Fruit Girl. The CLOWN *is seen at the window, and wants to buy fruit ;* HARLEQUIN *beckons him down ; the* CLOWN *obeys, and endeavours to steal the fruit ;* HARLEQUIN *prepares to treat him roughly.* PANTALOON *enters from the Inn, and intercedes for him ; the* CLOWN *is forgiven ; the* PANTALOON *pays him, and exit.* CLOWN *makes love to* NYMPH *; a dance is proposed,* (43) *when a mock opera by the* CLOWN *and* HARLEQUIN *; they both exit.* (44) *The scene changes.*

SCENE SIXTH.—*Inside of the Inn.*

(45) *The* LANDLORD *enters, followed by* SERVANTS, *who place chairs and a table covered, and exit.* HARLEQUIN *and* COLUMBINE *now enter and seat themselves ; they are surprised by the* CLOWN, *on whom* HARLEQUIN *plays tricks, and he runs off.* HARLEQUIN *rings the bell ; the* LANDLORD *enters ;* HARLEQUIN *asks for concealment ;* HARLEQUIN, COLUMBINE *and* LANDLORD *exeunt. The* CLOWN *enters, followed by* PANTALOON *and the* LANDLORD *; the two latter seat themselves, and are thrown off their chairs ; the* CLOWN *sits down at the table and drinks wine, and* PANTALOON *prepares to cut up a pie, when a live Duck flies out of it, and walks forward on the stage, to the surprise of* PANTALOON, *etc., the gratification of* CLOWN, *who, with mimic attitude, follows and seizes it, and runs off.* (46) HARLEQUIN *enters ;* PANTALOON *runs to the door and shuts it ; the* CLOWN *thrusts a chair at him, when* HARLEQUIN *leaps through some club rules ;* (47) PANTALOON *runs out of the door after him, which the* CLOWN *locks ; the* CLOWN *sits down to regale ;* HARLEQUIN *enters from the opposite door, waves his sword, and the magic table ascends ; the* CLOWN *for some time perceives not its situation, and narrowly examines, walking underneath and around where it stood ; he now looks up and sees the table, utters a shout of surprise, and quietly seats himself again, when the table descends and the* CLOWN *and chair go up ; he halloes ; instantly* PANTALOON *is heard knocking at the door ; the* LANDLORD *enters and opens it, when* PANTALOON *is struck with amazement at the* CLOWN'S *situation ; the* LANDLORD *exits, and returns with a saw to cut him down, during which time the chair and* CLOWN *have descended ; the* CLOWN *and* LANDLORD *seat themselves at the table, when it ascends gradually, and presents a first, a second, and a third tier of tables, covered with cloths, furnished exactly as the first, with two wax lights to each ; the* CLOWN *and* LANDLORD *separate them, when* PANTALOON, LANDLORD *and* CLOWN *place themselves at the respective tables, the* CLOWN *in the centre, and all three tables in a line* (48) *with* PANTALOON, CLOWN, *and* LANDLORD, *who ascend together to the height of six or seven feet, when the* CLOWN, *forgetful of his own situation, is laughing at his neighbour's.* HARLEQUIN *and* COLUMBINE *enter, when another table, to represent a small dining one, is brought on ;* HARLEQUIN *touches it, and a complete supper appears on it, lit up with six candles, at which instant the candles on the other three tables disappear ;* (49) HARLEQUIN *and* COLUMBINE

enjoy the elevated situation of their exalted friends, and exeunt. (50) SERVANTS *now appear, are equally surprised, when a humorous scene ensues, by the* CLOWN *pelting them with plates, etc., the* CLOWN *during this fracas catches a cocked hat, which has been thrown at him, puts it on, and appears the* PRESIDENT ODD FELLOW *of the high though not exactly free and easy situation.* Scene changes to

SCENE SEVENTH.—*View in a Market Town.*

(51) *A crowd of* VILLAGERS *enter, singing*

Chorus of the Country Fair.

CHORUS.   While pipes and tabors rend the air,
Neighbours, neighbours, haste to the fair.

(52) MORRIS DANCERS *now enter and exhibit.* (53) HARLEQUIN *and* COLUMBINE *enter, pursued, they claim protection of the* MORRIS DANCERS, *which they accede to.* (54) LANDLORD, PANTALOON, *and the* CLOWN *enter, they hustle them, walk on their hands with their heads downwards, which concludes this scene.* Scene changes to

SCENE EIGHTH.—*A Wood-cutter's Cottage.*

(55) *A* SAILOR-BOY *comes forward and sings the following :*

Song.

The sea was rough, the clouds were dark,
Far distant every joy,
When, forc'd by fortune to embark,
I went a cabin-boy.
My purse soon filled with foemen's gold,
I hastened home with joy ;
But wreck'd in sight of port, behold,
A hapless poor cabin-boy.

(56) *The* BOY *knocks at the cottage door, his* MOTHER *appears, and shortly after, the* WOOD-CUTTER *returning from labour, they exit into cottage.* (57) HARLEQUIN *and* COLUMBINE *enter, pursued ; they knock at the door,* WOOD-CUTTER *comes out, they entreat concealment, and their wish is gratified.* (58) *Shortly after, the* BEADLE *and* CONSTABLE *come to distrain the* WOOD-CUTTER'S *goods for rent,* BAILIFF *and* CONSTABLE *enter, they lament their hard fate, and* HARLEQUIN *condoles with them, finds he has no money about him, but suddenly recollecting his power, he changes a wheel that is seen on the stage to Fortune moving on her axis,* (59) *who disperses out her golden favours from her cornucopia, to the gratification and relief of the poor* WOOD-CUTTER *and Family. The* CLOWN *enters and as usual plunders from the Wood-cutter's* WIFE. HARLE-QUIN *drives him off.* HARLEQUIN *and* COLUMBINE *exit. The* WOOD-CUTTER, WIFE *and* BOY *exit. Change.*

143

SCENE NINTH.—*A Pavilion by Moonlight.*

(60) HARLEQUIN *and* COLUMBINE *enter, dance, etc. He changes two banks to a steel trap and spring gun. The* CLOWN *and* PANTALOON *enter. The* CLOWN *is caught by the trap,* (61) *the gun goes off, and frightens the* PANTALOON, *who leads off the* CLOWN *by the leg that is fastened in the trap, when the pavilion is changed by* HARLEQUIN *to*

SCENE TENTH.—*A Flower Garden.*

(62) GARDENERS *bring in three tubs with trees, the centre one of which is changed by* HARLEQUIN *to a sunflower, and* COLUMBINE *dances a pas seul.* (63) HARLEQUIN, *the* CLOWN *and* PANTALOON *appearing, changes the other two trees to the statues of himself and* COLUMBINE, (64) *behind which they conceal themselves,* (65) *the* CLOWN *knocks down* PANTALOON, *when* HARLEQUIN *links them together, and makes them turn round and round, over head and heels, in which way they exit.* HARLEQUIN *and* COLUMBINE *exit. Scene changes to*

SCENE ELEVENTH.—*A View of Golden Square.*

(66) *The* CLOWN *and* PANTALOON *enter. A house with lodgings to let attracts their attention.* PANTALOON *enters, and here a number of whimsical tricks between the* CLOWN *and* PANTALOON *are displayed by them. They exit into the house* (67). HARLEQUIN *and* COLUMBINE *enter ;* HARLEQUIN *knocks at the door, the* CLOWN *looks out of the window.* COLUMBINE *exit.* HARLEQUIN *waves his sword, and balcony falls,* (68) *a bustle ensues.* HARLEQUIN *exits ; the* CLOWN *and* PANTALOON *come out and exit. Change.*

SCENE TWELFTH.—*St. Dunstan's Church.*

(69) *A crowd are assembled to see the figures strike the bell, amongst whom is a pieman whom the* CLOWN *robs of his pies* (70). HARLEQUIN *and* COLUMBINE *enter, pursued ; he waves his sword. The dial descends, they place themselves on it, and are conveyed to the recess, where the two figures with clubs give place to them* (71). *The* CLOWN *and* PANTALOON *enter, view them with wonder.* HARLEQUIN *and* COLUMBINE *retire, and the two figures with clubs take their original situations. The* CLOWN *and* PANTALOON *appear entranced, and while they are lost in thought, a* JEW *enters ; they parley,* PANTALOON *bargains for two hats, during which time the* CLOWN *pilfers a jacket from the* JEW'S *bag, puts it on, and* JEW *exits. The dial again descends with the two figures who beat time with their clubs, terrifying* PANTALOON *and the* CLOWN, *whose hats are changed by* HARLEQUIN *into the two bells* (72). *The figures keep close to them, menacing to restore the bells, when* PANTALOON *mounts the dial and the* CLOWN *clings round it, ascending in this situation. Change.*

SCENE THIRTEENTH.—*Entrace to Vauxhall Gardens.*

(73) *Various characters now enter,* BEAUX, BELLES, *and a great variety of mixed company, attended by* WATERMEN, HACKNEY COACHMEN, LINK BOYS, *etc. The* CLOWN *enters and puts in practice his old tricks, he pilfers a* GENTLE-MAN *of his hat and a* LIGHT HORSEMAN *of his sword, when the following catch is sung :*

Catch.

VISITORS.	Here we are, we'll all be merry ;
	Vauxhall galas banish care :
WATERMEN.	Hope you'll please to pay the wherry—
COACHMEN.	Hope you'll pay poor coachee's fare.
1ST VISITOR.	Hang your nasty skulls and oars ;
2ND VISITOR.	Come, let's in and see the fun ;
1ST VISITOR.	What's to pay ? What monstrous bores ;
	What's your number ?
COACHMAN.	Three and sixpence !
1ST VISITOR.	I'll take care of No. 1 !
COACHMAN.	I'll summons you all,
WATERMAN.	To Waterman's Hall—
COACHMAN.	To Somerset House :
CHORUS.	A rare Vauxhall !

They all exeunt into gardens : changes to

SCENE FOURTEENTH.—*Orchestra in Vauxhall Gardens.* (74) *The orchestra is fully illuminated as on a gala night ; the* MUSICIANS *appear in motion ; the Company consists of great variety, and the illusion is completed by the entrance of the* PANDEAN MINSTRELS *playing the favourite air.*

The CLOWN *enters, and excites much laughter by playing on a large tin fish-kettle (which is hung round his neck) with a ladle and whisk, his chin resting on a hair broom, which he supports between his feet ; strikes up ;* (75) *the Company form a country dance,* (76) *after which the* CLOWN *throws the* WAITER *and Company into confusion by stealing table-cloths, etc.,* (77) *and a scene ensues full of merriment and fun—plates thrown in all directions, Fowls fly away off the dishes, etc., when the scene closes and all exeunt. Scene changes to*

SCENE FIFTEENTH.—*A Grocer's Shop and Post Office.*

(78) *The* CLOWN *enters and steals the letters out of the box ; he opens one and secretes some notes, then another,—" Sir, I'll trouble you with a line "— and exhibits a small card which is inclosed in a letter.* HARLEQUIN *enters, changes the letter-box into a lion's head. The* CLOWN *advances, puts his hand*

145

in to get more letters, and is caught fast in the mouth of the lion. He endeavours to extricate himself, and draws out of the box a little POSTMAN *(79) who annoys the* CLOWN *with his bell. A* BAKER *comes on, sets down his basket, and enters the grocer's shop. The* CLOWN *steals a loaf and throws it to* PANTALOON, *who now enters and covers the* POSTMAN *with the basket. While* PANTALOON *and the* CLOWN *are endeavouring to keep the basket over the* POSTMAN, *the top opens and a Blackamoor's Head appears and recedes. They are both terrified. The* CLOWN *goes in and returns with a board.* PANTALOON *pops upon one side of the basket, when the* CLOWN *breaks the board in two upon his head. They exit. Two* PORTERS *then bring in a chairman horse, on which are two chests of tea.* HARLEQUIN *and* COLUMBINE *enter, pursued, he changes the chests into an elegant sideboard, furnished complete, behind which he and* COLUMBINE *hide themselves.* HARLEQUIN *changes the scene to*

SCENE SIXTEENTH.—*Grocer's Parlour.*

(80) *The* CLOWN *and* PANTALOON *enter, and they drink wine with the magic bottle ; the* CLOWN *and* PANTALOON *go off.* HARLEQUIN *changes the sideboard into a beehive stand ; the whole of the scene, as if by magic, in one second presents the interior of*

SCENE SEVENTEENTH.—*A Farmyard.*

(81) HARLEQUIN *with* COLUMBINE *concealed behind the bee stand, (82) when* PANTALOON *and the* CLOWN *enter, each takes up a beehive ; the bees swarm about their heads, and they exeunt, bellowing. The scene now changes to*

SCENE EIGHTEENTH.—*The Mermaid's Cave ; (83) the perspective shews the sea through the opening of the cavern.*

MOTHER GOOSE *enters, attended by four* FAIRIES, *whom she addresses in these lines :*

> Your task concludes, your mistress' rage is o'er,
> These wandering mortals, I'll perplex no more,
> Go wake the favourite of my sprites, who sleep
> Within the briny bosom of the deep ;
> The spell-bound egg, from bondage to redeem,
> Reward true love, and end our magic dream.

(84) MOTHER GOOSE *and* FAIRIES *exit (85) when* ODDFISH *rises out of the sea. Pantomime for* ODDFISH *(86). Comes forward smacking the serpents that twine around his legs, and takes up two shells and devours the fish. He then exits (87).* HARLEQUIN *with* COLUMBINE *enters, as also soon after* ODDFISH. COLUMBINE *is terrified, and* HARLEQUIN *pours wine into the mouth of* ODDFISH

146

from his sword (88). HARLEQUIN *now commands him to dive into the sea for the golden egg, he obeys, and returns with a seaweed* (89) *which* COLUMBINE *receives ; he goes a second time, and comes forward with the golden egg,* (90) HARLEQUIN *receives it from him.* (91) CLOWN *and* PANTALOON *enter.* HARLEQUIN *and* COLUMBINE *take shelter behind* ODDFISH, *who keeps each at bay with his serpents.* MOTHER GOOSE *enters* (92). HARLEQUIN *presents to her the golden egg, and she reconciles all parties with these lines :*

MOTHER G.   The egg returned, receive thy lovely choice,
The gift is sanctioned by her guardian's voice.
You soon restored to person, house, and lands,
Shall like a hearty English squire, shake hands.
Meanwhile his magic dwelling you shall view,
Furnished by fairy hands, to pleasure you.

(93) MOTHER GOOSE *waves her stick. Changes to a view of the last scene, representing*

SCENE NINETEENTH.—*A Submarine Palace,*

The wings and sides of which are dolphins ; in the perspective a tripod of them, and two recesses or alcoves, in each of which is seen a MERMAID *busily employed in combing her hair, and the whole terminated by a distant view of the sea.* DANCERS *approach habited to correspond with the scene, and at the finale, the* SQUIRE *joins the lovers' hands.*

CHORUS.—MOTHER GOOSE, SQUIRE, PANTALOON, etc.

(95) *Finale.*

MOTHER G.   Ye patrons kind, who deign to view
The sports our scenes produce,
Accept our wish to pleasure you,
And laugh with Mother Goose.

CHORUS.   And laugh with Mother Goose, etc.

SQUIRE.   And let no critic stern reject
What our petitions beg,
That we may from your smiles collect
Each night some Golden Egg.

FULL CHORUS.   Ye patrons kind, who deign to view
The sport we'd fain produce,
Accept our wish to pleasure you,
And laugh with Mother Goose.

147

MOTHER G.   Who humbly begs,
                        On bended legs,
                        That you, God lack,
                        Her cause will back,
                        And scorn to crack
                        Her Golden Egg.

FULL CHORUS.   Who humbly begs, etc.

CURTAIN.

148

Index

Index

INDEX

INDEX

INDEX

INDEX

154

INDEX

INDEX